Introduction

A look into history

Metals are probably the most important group of materials in our lives. It was not until man discovered metals that he was able to advance towards a civilised existence. Without this discovery we might never have developed beyond the Stone Age.

We must remember, though, that primitive man probably discovered metals by accident. It is interesting to wonder how this could have happened. We don't know exactly, but it could be that a fire was made on top of some rock or earth that contained metal ore. The glowing wood embers could then have caused globules of metal to form underneath the fire. If the man who made the fire was very observant, he could have discovered one of the materials which we now call a metal.

Now imagine that you are this man. You are sitting by the fire in your cave and have discovered this new material. You can see that

Figure 1 The proportion by weight of the elements in the earth's crust. The key below the graph gives the proportions as percentages.

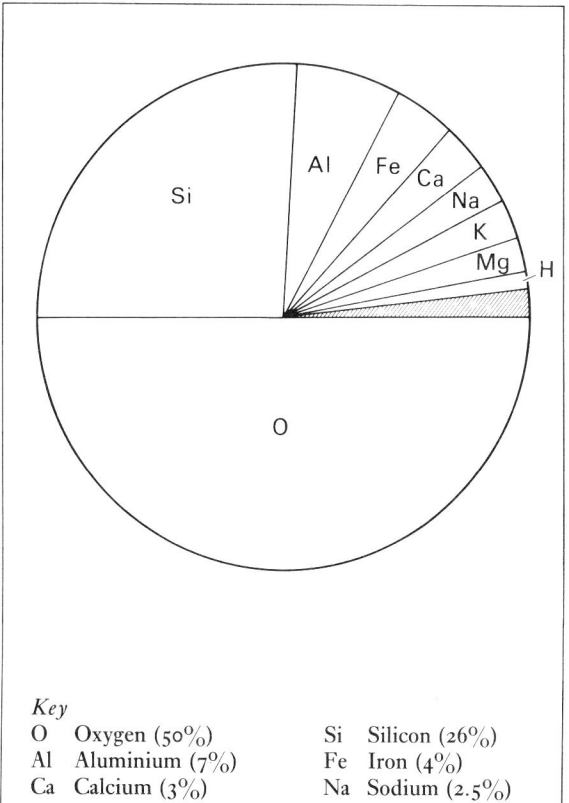

Key

O	Oxygen (50%)	Si	Silicon (26%)
Al	Aluminium (7%)	Fe	Iron (4%)
Ca	Calcium (3%)	Na	Sodium (2.5%)
K	Potassium (2.5%)	Mg	Magnesium (2%)
H	Hydrogen (1%)		

Figure 2 The relative proportions of the metals found in the earth's crust. The key gives the amount in parts per million of each metal in the earth's crust.

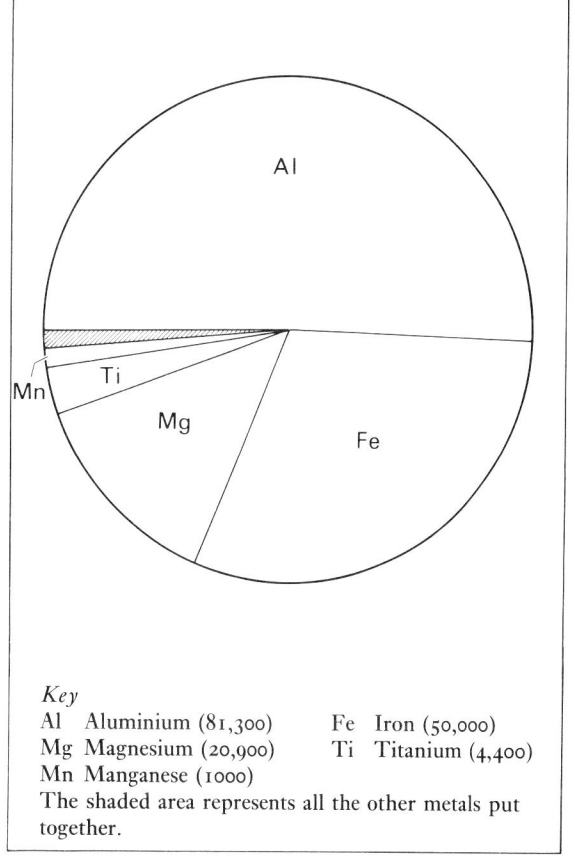

Key

Al	Aluminium (81,300)	Fe	Iron (50,000)
Mg	Magnesium (20,900)	Ti	Titanium (4,400)
Mn	Manganese (1000)		

The shaded area represents all the other metals put together.

3

Figure 3 The relative proportions of the 'other metals' referred to in Figure 2. They amount to only 1063 parts per million of the earth's crust.

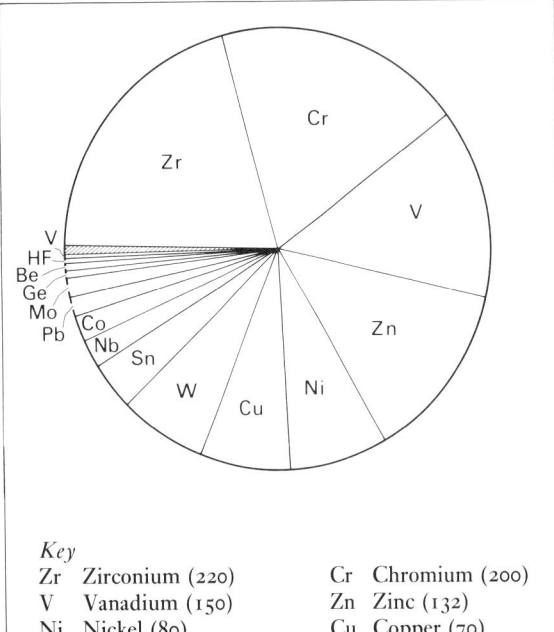

Key

Zr Zirconium (220)	Cr Chromium (200)
V Vanadium (150)	Zn Zinc (132)
Ni Nickel (80)	Cu Copper (70)
W Tungsten (69)	Sn Tin (40)
Nb Niobium (24)	Co Cobalt (23)
Pb Lead (16)	Mo Molybdenum (15)
Ge Germanium (7)	Be Beryllium (6)
Hf Hafnium (4.5)	U Uranium (4)

The shaded area represents *all* the remaining metals, which include gold, silver and platinum. This total amounts to only 2.5 parts per million.

there isn't very much of it, but when it cools down you can also see that it could be very useful to you, just as stone and wood are. In what way do you think it would be most useful to you? Could you use it to make tools, so that you could build and make things more easily? Or would it be more useful to make weapons for hunting? Still imagining that you are a primitive man, can you think of any other use for this new material?

A look around today

Today we know that there are about seventy different metals. But we use only about half of these, and some of them in very small quantities. We use small amounts of some metals to make alloys, which are 'mixtures' of different metals.

About a quarter of the earth's crust consists of metals. Figures 1, 2 and 3 give more information about the quantities of the different metals found in the earth's crust.

Look around you and see what metals you can spot. There are metals everywhere, but two good places to start looking would be the kitchen and under the bonnet of a car. At first glance you may have difficulty deciding which substances are metals and which are not. If you are in doubt, rub lightly with some steel wool; metals are *shiny*.

Notice what the metals are used for and try to decide why each particular metal was chosen for each particular job. To help decide this, try to work out what properties the metal possesses. Is it perhaps hard, soft, or brittle? You can write down your findings on a chart, like this:

Metal	
Where used	
Why used	
Pure metal or alloy	

You may find it difficult to decide what to put in the last line. What exactly is an alloy? We hope that this book will help you to answer that question and many others concerning the very important group of substances called the metals.

Metals

Bob Farr

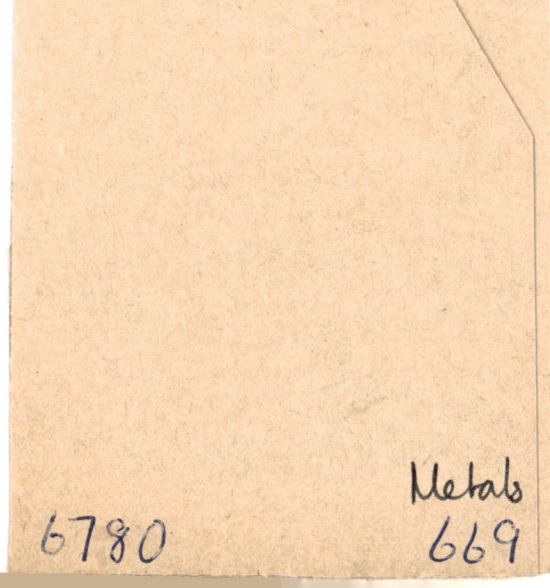

Evans Brothers Limited London

Published by Evans Brothers Ltd., Montague House,
Russell Square, London W.C.1.

Acknowledgements
Cover photograph by courtesy of RTZ Services Ltd.

Cartoons by Ewan McLeish.

Artwork by Cartographic Enterprises.

British Aircraft Corporation, Fig. 4; Ford Motor Co.,
Figs. 9, 40; GKN Sankey Ltd., Fig. 10; Chamber of
Mines of South Africa, Figs. 15, 47, 48; Planair Ltd.,
Fig. 16; Aluminium Federation Ltd., Figs. 17, 18, 20;
Alcan Industries Ltd., Fig. 19; Visual Planning Systems
Ltd., Fig. 21; British Rail, Fig. 22; The London
Planetarium, Fig. 24; Copper Development Association,
Figs. 25, 26, 27, 28, 29, 30; British Steel Corporation,
Figs. 32, 33, 34, 35, 36, 37, 38, 39; U.K. Atomic Energy
Authority, Fig. 42; Lead Development Association, Figs.
43, 44, 45; RTZ Services Ltd., Figs. 49, 50, 51; Zinc
Development Association, Fig. 52; Derbyshire Evening
Telegraph, Fig. 41.

General Editor of the SCIENCE IN FOCUS series
John May B.Sc.(Agric), M.Phil., M.I.Biol.

Contents

Filmset by Photoprint Plates Ltd., Rayleigh, Essex.
Printed in Great Britain by
BAS Printers Limited, Wallop, Hampshire
ISBN 0 237 28990 3

The Physical Properties of Metals

Some metals are used for particular jobs because of their special physical properties—because they are hard or soft, light or heavy, for example. Iron is used for the sides of ships because it is tough. But it is too heavy to be used in aeroplanes, so the much lighter metal, aluminium, is used. Figure 4 shows the fuselage of Concorde 002 under construction at Weybridge.

Each metal is different in some way from all the others, but all metals have some properties in common. You can make your own experiments to test some of these properties. If you work with friends you will be able to test more metals and compare results.

First of all you need as many different metals as possible. They will almost certainly be damaged during the experiments, so do not use something that you may want again.

Here are some ideas for what you could use:
Aluminium—an old saucepan or frying pan
Lead—a piece of lead piping
Copper—a piece of copper piping or the 'ball' from an old lavatory cistern
Iron—'any old iron', but a piece about the same thickness as your aluminium would be best
Zinc—an old toy car.

You can of course add other metals to this list, and also any other materials which you want to test to see if they are made of metal.

Figure 4 Concorde 002 under construction at Weybridge

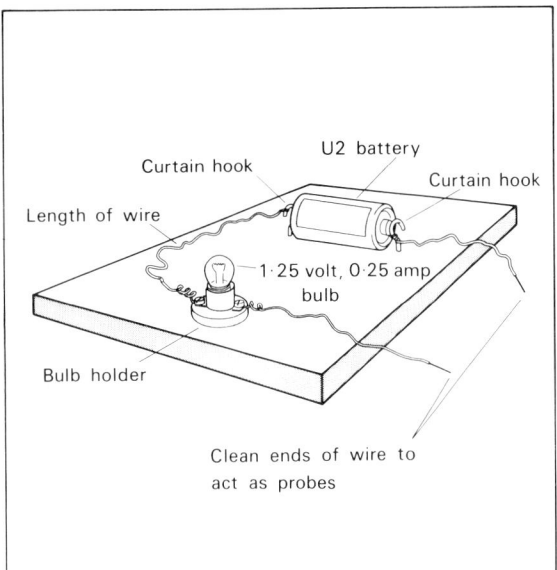

Figure 5 Apparatus for testing the electrical conductivity of metals

1 Electrical conductivity: For this investigation you will need:

a One torch battery, U.2 type
b Three pieces of wire, 10 cm long
c A bulb holder
d A 1.25 volt, 0.25 amp torch bulb
e Two metal curtain hooks
f A piece of wood, approximately 30 cm wide, 20 cm long and 1 cm thick

Mount the various items on the piece of wood. The diagram (Figure 5) will help you with the layout of the items.

Two of the pieces of wire are going to be your probes. When you bring them together the bulb lights, because you complete the circuit.

Now you can test whether each item in your collection of materials conducts electricity. You do this by touching each item with the two probes. If the bulb lights, then the material conducts electricity.

Note: you must make a good contact between the probes and the material you are testing (metal, plastic or cloth) if your results are to mean anything. To make sure of this, rub lightly with wire wool at the points on the material where you are going to place the probes.

2 Thermal conductivity: In order to test the thermal conductivity of metals—that is,

whether or not they conduct heat—you will need:

a Pieces of different metals about 10 cm long and of about the same thickness
b A candle
c A ball-bearing
d Somebody to help you
e A watch

Stick the ball-bearing on the end of the piece of metal with a little candle wax. Now your helper must press the unwaxed end of the piece of metal on a table or bench while you warm it about 3 cm from the fixed end. The diagram (Figure 6) will help you.

See what happens to the ball-bearing in each case. What second general property does this tell you that metals share?

If you *time* how long it takes for the ball-bearing to fall off the different pieces of metal, you will see why aluminium is used to make saucepans and frying pans. Why don't we use copper? Later on in the book you will discover why.

3 Hardness: You will need:

a Your pieces of metal and other materials
b A ball-bearing

Simply drop your ball-bearing from the same height on to each material in turn and notice the height to which it bounces. Make sure that the piece of material is securely fixed down before you start.

This investigation should tell you a third general property that all metals share. Why do you think lead is used in pipes, and iron in knives and forks?

4 Malleability: Cut or hacksaw a piece about 1 cm square from each of your metals. Hammer each piece on a hard surface. What happens to the pieces of metal? Do they all behave in the same way? Do the same with a piece of wood or plastic.

Substances which can be hammered or pressed out of their original form without a tendency to return to it or to fracture are described as *malleable*. All metals are malleable. You will have noticed that not all are equally so. Can you put them in order of malleability? One of your five metals is often used in the form of a thin sheet. Which one? (You might

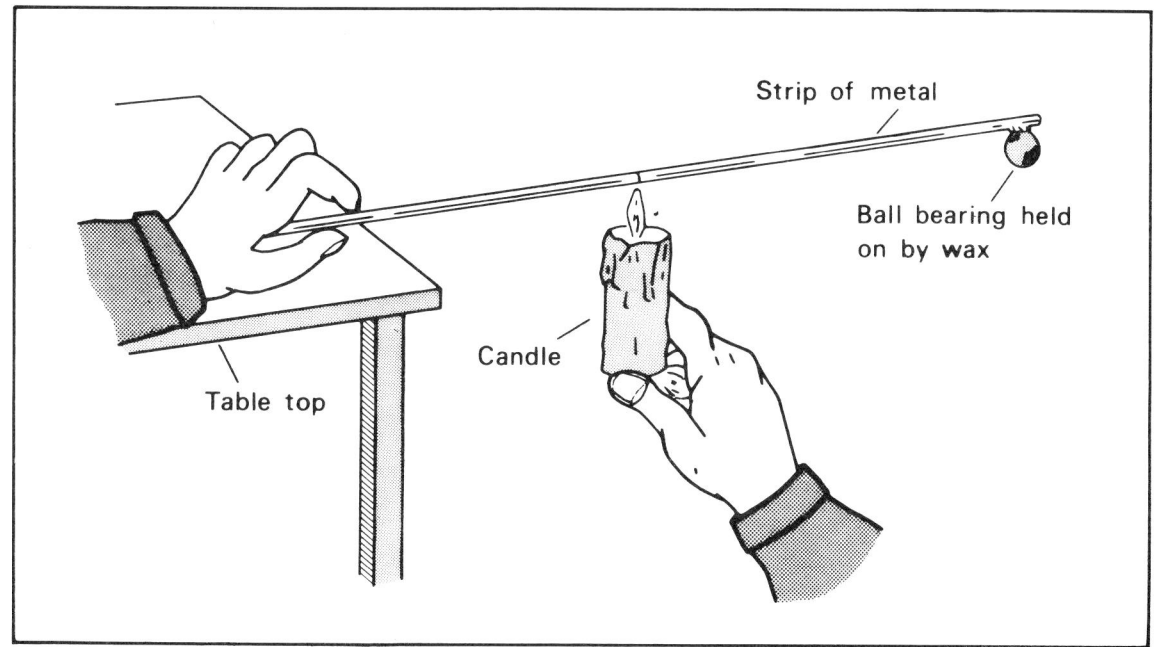

Figure 6 Apparatus for testing the thermal conductivity of metals

have found a thin sheet of this metal in the kitchen.)

5 'Bendability': This is very easy to test. Take a piece of metal in your hands and try to bend it. Do all the metals bend easily? Do they revert to their original state after you have bent them a little? What happens after more severe bending?

Try similar experiments with pieces of plastic, wood, slate or any other non-metal you can find.

Does the differing 'bendability' of the various metals influence the uses to which they are put?

6 Ductility: Many metals can be drawn out into thin wires and this property is called ductility.

7 Density: You may have noticed that, for samples of equal size, lead is heavier than iron, and that iron is heavier than aluminium. How heavy are copper and zinc compared with other metals?

All these metals are heavier than most non-metals you can find—size for size, that is.

The heaviness is called the *density* of the substance. A standard size for quoting densities of 1 cubic centimetre (1 cm^3) is internationally

agreed, and the mass of that volume is often given in tables in text and reference books.

A list of the densities of several common substances is given below. Each is in grammes per cubic centimetre, g/cm^3.

a *Metals*

Aluminium 2.7	Copper 8.9	Lead 11.4
Iron 7.9	Nickel 8.9	Gold 19.3
Mercury 13.6	Zinc 7.1	

b *Non-metals*

| Hard-wood 0.6 | Soft-wood 0.5 | Glass 2.4 |
| Slate 2.9 | Marble 2.7 | Perspex 1.1 |

It was this property of metals that enabled old-time miners to find gold by the method called panning. This consisted of agitating the earth containing the gold specks in a continuous stream of running water. The lighter, rocky material was washed away, leaving behind specks of the heavier gold.

In Malaysia some tin ore is still obtained by a similar method.

The heaviness of certain metals is mainly due to the structure of the nucleus of their atoms. The arrangement of these atoms in crystal forms is very important to the physical properties of the metal.

The Physical Properties of Metals and their Crystal Structure

Use a magnifying glass to look at some grains of salt. Then look at castor sugar (which is very fine and used for baking), ordinary sugar and brown sugar. You will be looking at crystals.

If you look at soot or baking powder in the same way, you will see that this is different. Not all things are made up of crystals.

When you look at the three kinds of sugar you will see that the same substance can be made from different-shaped crystals. The shape of the crystals affects the physical properties of

the substance. The crystals of metals are very different from those of sugar, and their shape has a major influence on the properties of the particular metal.

It is much more difficult to see the crystals in metals than in sugar. Many metal articles are polished or burnished when they are manufactured, and this makes it difficult to see the crystal shapes. But sometimes you *can* see them: good places to look are new dustbins and the parts of metal toys that have not been painted. In both cases you are likely to see the flat surfaces of zinc crystals. Metal crystals such

Figure 7 The three basic metal crystal structures

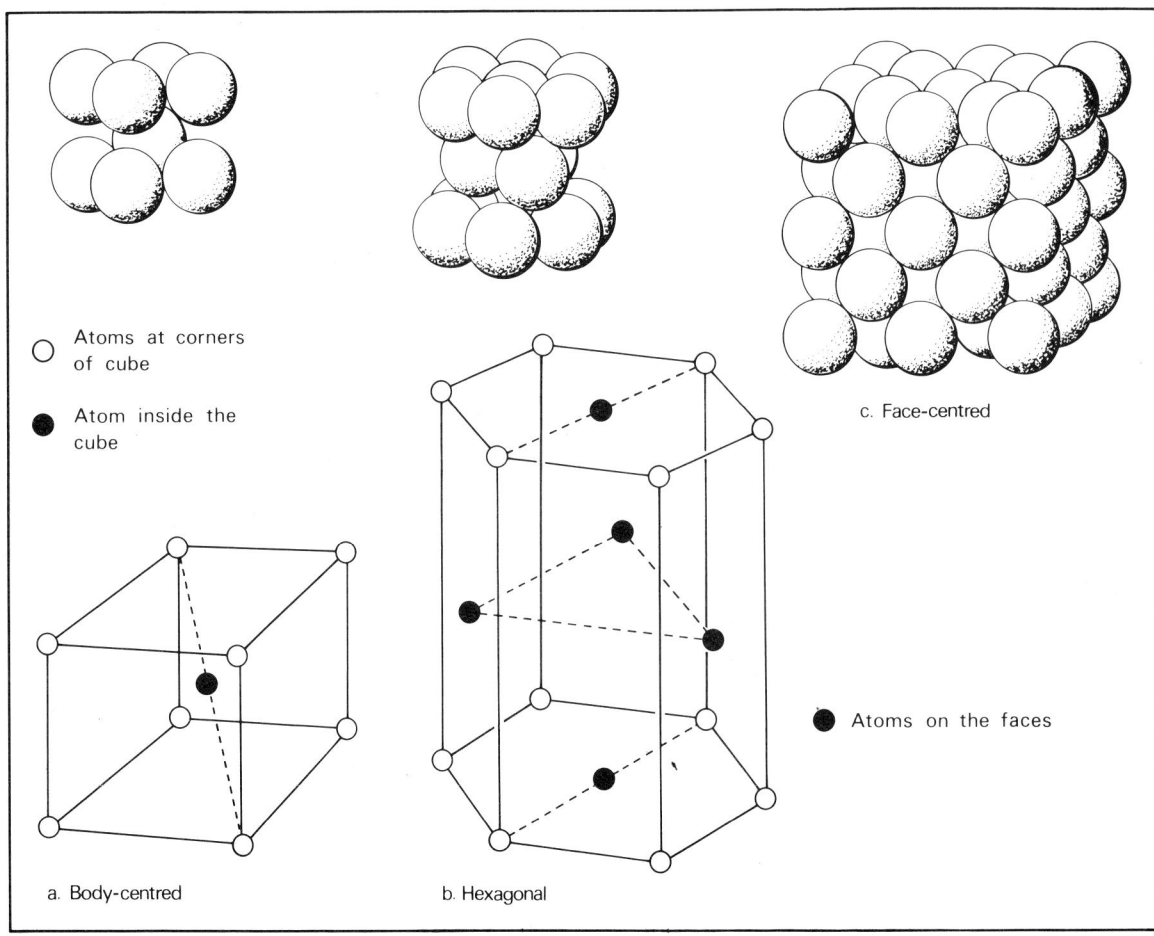

○ Atoms at corners of cube

● Atom inside the cube

c. Face-centred

● Atoms on the faces

a. Body-centred   b. Hexagonal

'. . . good places to look for zinc crystals are new dustbins . . .'

as those on the new dustbin can be quite large—several centimetres across. Neither the outer edges of metal crystals nor their faces are as regular and smooth as those in salt or sugar, but the way the atoms are packed is just as regular.

The three basic patterns formed by crystals are shown in Figure 7. The atoms in the crystal structure are held in position and linked by bonds. When you bend a piece of metal so that its shape is permanently altered, these bonds are broken and a slip takes place. Then the bonds re-establish themselves in a new position.

The dislocations produced by the slip can be strengthened by adding another metal to make an *alloy*. This stops slipping because the atoms of the second metal dissolve and implant themselves in the crystal, and help to prevent the spread of dislocations. In this way the physical properties of the metal are improved. A good example is brass—an alloy of copper and up to 30% zinc. The alloy is much stronger than either pure copper or pure zinc.

All different methods of altering the hardness of a metal such as heat, work hardening, or surface treatment are effective because they bring about changes in its crystal structure.

This can be shown in an experiment you could do with the help of your teacher, using an old steel knitting needle. First of all try bending it. It will be hard, tough and springy and will not bend easily. Now heat one end of it to red heat in a gas flame and allow it to cool slowly. Be careful because, as you now know, metals conduct heat and the other end will get hot. If you try bending it after it has cooled you will see it is softer.

Now heat one end again, but this time plunge it into cold water to cool it. Attempts at bending it will show that it is now brittle. Clean up the brittle piece and warm it slowly a few centimetres above a flame. Then put it into water. This time it will be similar to how it was when you started.

It is the same needle, made from the same material. What you have done shows that the way you treat a metal can change its physical properties. The changes occur because the treatment affects the structure of the metal crystals—causing or stopping slips or dislocations.

If we influence the crystal structure, then we also affect physical properties of the metal. This means that we can make metals hard, soft or brittle according to what they will be used for.

The Chemical Properties of Metals

When we talk about the chemical properties of a substance we mean those properties which influence its behaviour and interactions with other substances.

The chemical properties of a metal are very important. They affect both the uses to which the metal can be put and the form in which the metal is found in the earth's surface.

First of all, we will look at the use of the metal. For example, the tendency of a metal to corrode—that is, to combine with oxygen or other substances from the air—will influence the uses to which it is put. The fact that a metal has corroded shows that a chemical reaction has taken place, and so the tendency to corrode is a chemical property.

Secondly, we shall examine how the chemical properties of a metal influence the form in which it is found. In the high temperature found in the earth's crust many millions of years ago, most metals reacted chemically with other elements to form the compounds from which we have to extract them today. Exceptions were gold and platinum, which are found native—that is, uncombined in any way and usually found as tiny specks of the pure metal. The capacity of the metal to react with other elements in the earth's crust to form mineral ores is an example of a chemical reaction arising from a chemical property of the metal.

Reactivity: The tendency or capacity to form new compounds differs from metal to metal and is called its *reactivity*.

Burning: If you put a milk bottle top into a fire it will burn completely and form dust. This dust is aluminium oxide, for the aluminium of the milk bottle top has reacted with oxygen in the air. If you now do the same with a piece of copper it will glow red-hot, but when you take it out of the fire you will find that it has not burned completely, but has a thin black coating on it which will easily peel off. This is a coating of copper oxide, the copper having reacted with oxygen.

We have now seen that aluminium and copper behave differently when they are heated. Aluminium forms oxide more readily than copper. This is because aluminium is more reactive than copper.

If we make a list of common metals in order of reactivity, it looks like this:

Magnesium
Aluminium
Zinc
Iron
Tin
Lead
Copper.

We can put our knowledge of the metals' degree of reactivity to many uses. For example, because we know that aluminium is more reactive than iron, we can work out that, if aluminium powder is mixed with iron oxide powder and heated, a reaction will take place. This is because the aluminium will react with the oxygen in iron oxide to form aluminium oxide. In this case the iron will be left behind.

The reaction takes place because of the difference between the chemical properties of the two metals. This kind of reaction takes place in some fireworks.

Very important is the fact that the non-metal carbon can be put high in this order of reactivity. It is used in the form of coke and burned wood to take the oxygen out of ores in the manufacture of metals such as iron and zinc as we shall see later.

Reactivity and oxidation: It might seem confusing at first sight that iron seems to go rusty quickly, but aluminium, which is more reactive, does not.

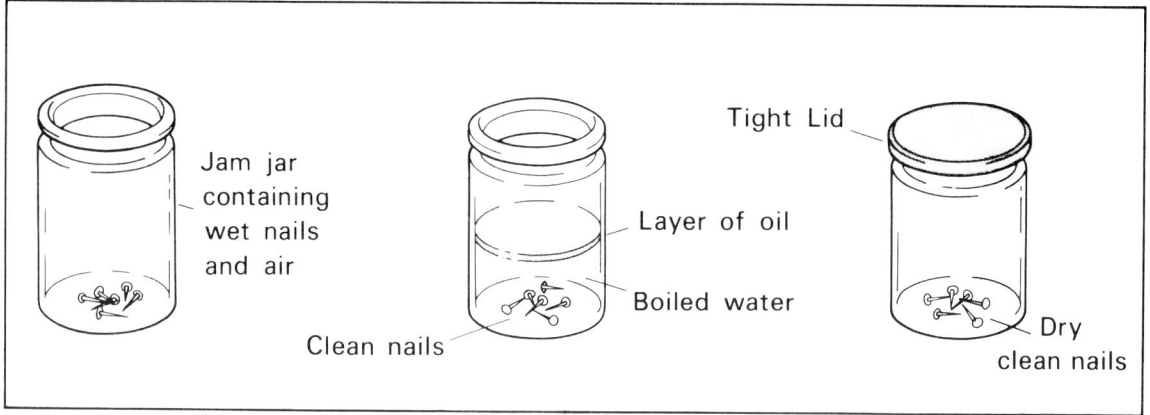

Figure 8 Apparatus for investigating under what conditions iron rusts.

When substances react with oxygen this is called oxidation. Iron oxidises quickly to form rust (iron III oxide). This flakes off and more oxidation then takes place, the process repeating itself until the piece of iron breaks up. It is the fact that the flakes of rust fall off that is all-important. Aluminium oxidises much more quickly than iron to form aluminium oxide but the coating of aluminium oxide does not flake off. It stays as a thin coating and protects the rest of the aluminium from the oxygen in the air, and thus from further oxidation. If mercury is rubbed onto a piece of aluminium, it stops this coating from protecting the aluminium, which then reacts so fast that hair-like growths of aluminium oxide can be seen forming.

Protecting iron from corrosion: We mentioned that iron rusts easily. But under what conditions does it rust? Set up the investigation shown in Figure 8 which will help you to find out. The results will help you to decide what to do to prevent iron from rusting.

The oil on top of the boiled water stops any air dissolving in the water. Look at the nails at the end of a day, a week and a month. The investigation gives you a clue to the *two* main factors which control rusting.

Rusting is a very complicated process. The results of your investigation should enable you to think out why the various methods of rust prevention are used.

Now we'll look more closely at five of these methods: painting; coating with another metal;

greasing or oiling; plastic spray; cathodic protection.

Painting: You may have seen photographs of the Forth Railway Bridge being painted, usually with a caption telling you that it is a never-ending job. As the men finish at one end they start again at the other. If they had not done this since the bridge was built it would have corroded and fallen into the water by now.

Not all paints are good at preventing iron from rusting. You can experiment by coating nails with different kinds of paint and leaving them in water.

Types you might use are: emulsion paint; ordinary gloss paint; poly-urethane gloss paint; cellulose (car) paint; primer paint; lead base paint; bitumastic paint.

If you now coat two clean nails with each paint, then add a coat of poly-urethane varnish to one of them and put them in water again, you will discover something else.

The investigations may give you a clue as to why certain types of paints are used for under-sealing cars, for example. But they will also show you that most paints do not stop rust; they only slow up the process of rust setting in. Figure 9 shows a car body being dip-painted with undercoat. The top coat will be sprayed on later. Do you think these coats of paint will stop the car body from rusting?

Coating with another metal: This is one of the best ways of preventing rust. The coating is usually put on by electrolysis (electrolytic deposition) and the cheapest of these methods is *galvanising*. This consists of dipping the iron in molten zinc. Zinc is only slightly more

Figure 9 A car body being dip-painted

reactive than iron, but, like aluminium, it forms a thin coat of oxide which stops further oxidation. Dustbins or garage roofs are often made of galvanised iron.

A second, and more expensive way is to coat the iron with tin. This is very effective because tin is not very reactive. The containers which we call tins are, in fact, iron coated with an extremely thin layer of tin. The layer is made thin because tin is a costly metal.

A third, and even more expensive method is chromium-plating. This is achieved by an electrical process called electrolysis, and is quite complicated. Usually, coatings of copper and nickel are deposited onto the iron by electrolysis and then the shiny chromium is added. The thicker the layers, the more expensive the job, but the better it is. The chromium on the bumper of a Rolls-Royce does not show signs of rust as easily or as quickly as that on a cheaper car. Figure 10 shows chromium-plated car bumper bars.

The cost of cars being attacked by rust runs into many millions of pounds each year, because cellulose paint does not give much long-term protection. Do you think it would be worth galvanising the whole of the car, even if it added £10 or £20 to the cost?

All the methods of coating iron with another metal depend on stopping contact between the iron and oxygen and water. The thicker the coating of the other metal, the more effective, but expensive, the method. A balance has to be made with cost very much in mind. It is also as well to realise that it is useless to employ this method if the coating is likely to be scratched at all. Why is this?

Greasing or oiling: This is one of the easiest and cheapest methods of rust prevention. Like the previous method, greasing or oiling a metal is successful because it places a barrier between the metal and oxygen and water. The restrictions on its use are obvious—it is rather messy—but it is very useful for protecting iron parts while they are being stored, or standing in water. For example, if you lay up your bicycle

Figure 10 Chromium-plated bumper bars

for the winter, a coating of oil will stop its bright parts from rusting.

Using a plastic spray: Here again, the method depends on putting an effective barrier between the metal and the rusting agents. It is a fairly expensive method and so it is not used very often. It also has the disadvantage that the plastic tends to chip, leaving areas where oxygen and water can attack the metal.

Cathodic protection: The principle of cathodic protection can be shown by a simple experiment that you can do yourself; the diagram (Figure 11) will help.

The metals are put into damp soil. The iron connected to the aluminium will not rust, but the aluminium will corrode. This is because chemicals dissolved in the water present in the damp soil cause an electrical cell to be set up. Electricity flows between the two metals, via the connecting wire and the minerals dissolved in the soil water.

In recent years, ironwork of many kinds has been protected from rust by this method, but its most important use has been on ships. Slabs of zinc are fixed to the hull of a ship for this purpose (see Figure 52 on page 59). The salt water provides the electrolyte for the electrical cell and the slabs corrode. The cost of these slabs is relatively small compared with the cost of rust damage.

Metals, their reactivity, and the production of electricity

In the eighteenth century two scientists, Luigi Galvani and Alesandro Volta, were discussing various things to do with what we now know as electricity. Galvani had discovered that a dead frog's leg twitched if it was lying on a zinc plate and was touched with a knife. Volta experimented and came to the conclusion that this was an electrical effect, owing to the presence of two different metals, connected via the chemicals in the frog's legs.

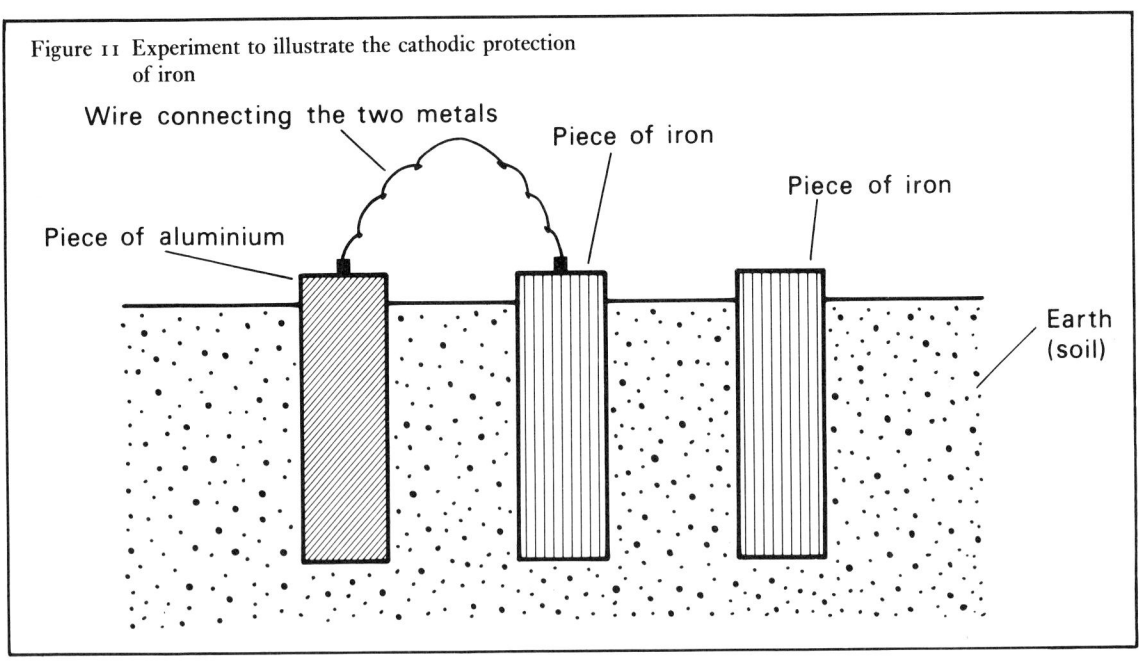

Figure 11 Experiment to illustrate the cathodic protection of iron

Wire connecting the two metals

Piece of iron

Piece of iron

Piece of aluminium

Earth (soil)

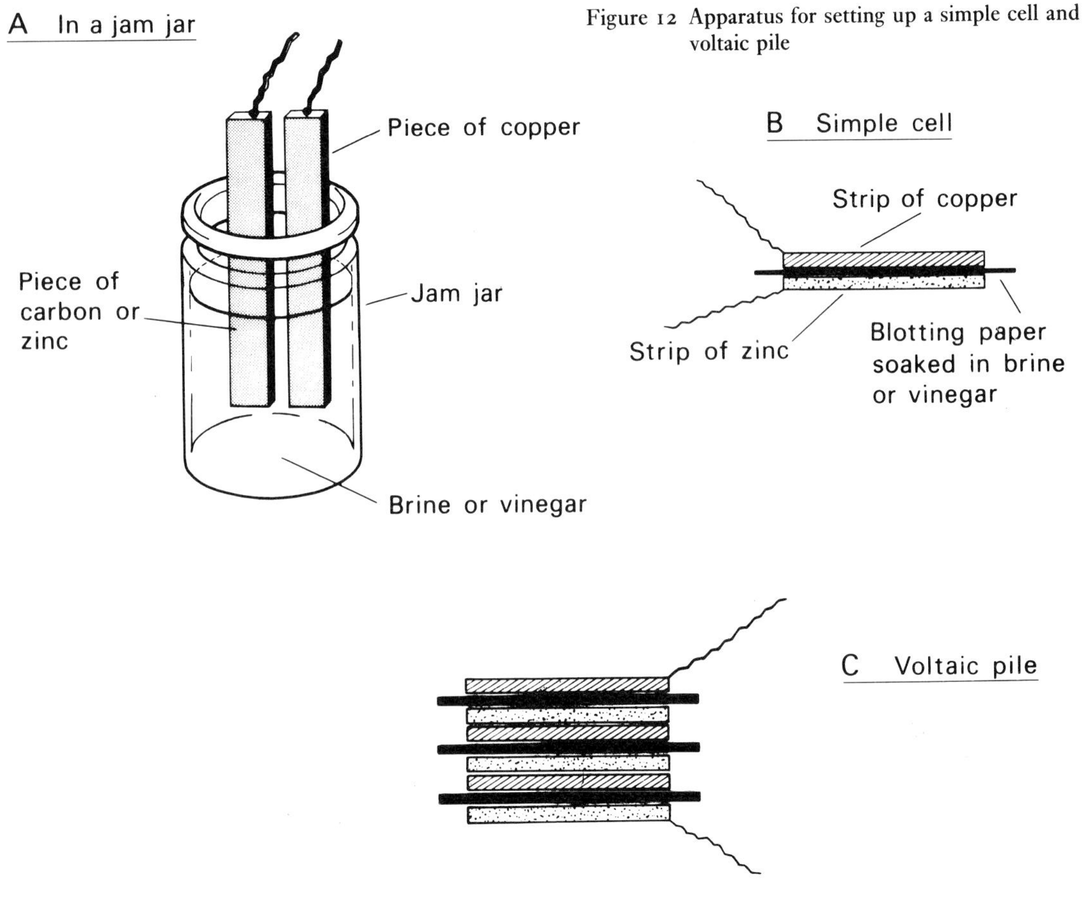

A   In a jam jar

Figure 12 Apparatus for setting up a simple cell and voltaic pile

Piece of copper

B   Simple cell

Strip of copper

Piece of carbon or zinc

Jam jar

Strip of zinc

Blotting paper soaked in brine or vinegar

Brine or vinegar

C   Voltaic pile

Volta went on to make the forerunner of today's torch batteries, or cells, and the pile cells that are used in some transistor radios.

You can easily construct such cells yourself. You just need two different metals and a suitable liquid. It has been found that acids and salts, dissolved in water, are best for this purpose. You could use any of these:

vinegar—acetic acid
lemon juice—citric acid
vitamin C tablets—ascorbic acid
common salt—sodium chloride.

The liquid is called an *electrolyte*. Figure 12B shows you how to make a single cell, and 12C a pile cell. You can see if electricity is being produced by connecting the cell to a torch bulb. One cell may not give enough electricity to light it up, so make a pile of first two, then three cells, and so on.

Volta's work was carried on by other scientists, such as Daniell and Leclanché, who designed and developed more cells. These were based on the same principle, but it was found that carbon could be used as one of the plates. In all cases the plates (metals or carbon) are used up as electricity is taken from the cell. You can try this with an ordinary torch battery. Just connect the bobble end to the flat back end with a piece of wire, and leave for a day or so. You will find that the outer case of zinc dissolves and that white paste oozes out. This paste is the electrolyte of the cell, and is a salt called ammonium chloride.

The diagram (Figure 13) shows you the construction of a torch cell. It is sometimes called a dry cell, because it is a drier version of the cell developed by Leclanché. You can quite safely saw one up, and examine the contents. Do the same with a transistor battery, and you will see that its principle is the same as Volta's pile of cells.

Any pair of dissimilar metals, when placed in an electrolyte, will produce electricity. You can try your metals with the electrolytes mentioned. Figure 12A will help you set up this experiment. You may well find that some pairs of metals do not light up the bulb when they are in similar-sized piles to other pairs. The greatest *voltage* is obtained from metals (and carbon) that are farthest apart in the reactivity list. You may have trouble when using aluminium, as it has to

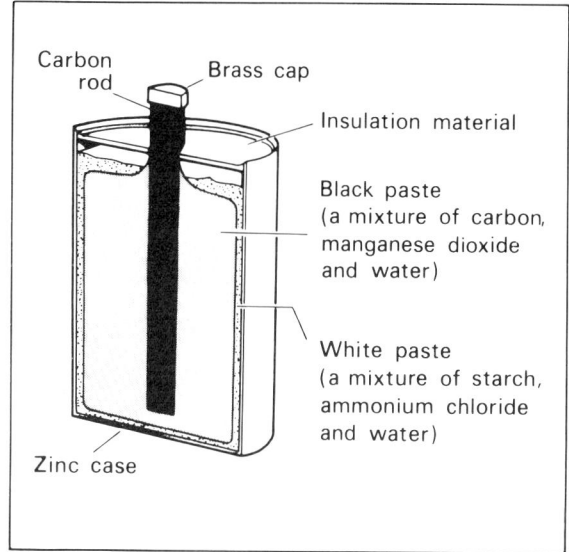

Figure 13 Section of a torch battery

be chemically pure. This is difficult to achieve as aluminium so easily forms a coat of oxide.

Voltages obtained from pairs of different metals are:

Aluminium	—Copper	1.6 volts
Zinc	—Copper	1.1 volts
Iron	—Copper	0.8 volts
Zinc	—Lead	0.6 volts
Lead	—Copper	0.4 volts

The car battery is different from the cells we have already looked at. The most important difference is that it can be re-charged. In fact, it is constantly being re-charged while the car is running. The second difference is that the plates of the cells are made of the same basic material—lead. When it is being re-charged, one of these plates (the one we call the positive) is changed to lead oxide. In this way the two plates become different and can then give a voltage. Whilst the car battery (a pile of these lead and lead oxide plates) is giving off a voltage, or discharging, the positive plate changes back to lead.

So the car battery, like the other cells above, produces its electrical energy from chemical energy.

The electrolyte in a car battery is sulphuric acid which should be handled with care.

The Metals: an Earth Resource

As mentioned in the Introduction, of the ninety or so elements that occur naturally in the earth's crust, seventy are metals. As man's technological capacity has increased he has discovered how to extract and use more metals. About eighteen of the metals are in general use, and six of these have many uses and particular importance for us.

As man's understanding of metals increases, and his methods of extracting them develop, certain of today's lesser-known metals will be used more and more. Examples are titanium—which is quite abundant in the earth's crust, but difficult to extract—and zirconium. Demand will play a part in this too. Zirconium is needed for nuclear reactors, and so is being increasingly extracted—but at a high cost.

The cost of extracting some of these 'rarer' metals can be reduced by increasing their usage and by employing better extraction methods. The importance of this will become greater as the more common metals are used up. The table below gives the expectation of life of known deposits of some common metals at the *present* rate of world consumption—but remember that the rate of consumption is increasing every year.

Figure 14 Where metallic minerals are found

Aluminium	Al	Mercury	Hg
Chromium	Cr	Nickel	Ni
Cobalt	Co	Platinum	Pt
Copper	Cu	Silver	Ag
Gold	Au	Tin	Sn
Iron	Fe	Titanium	Ti
Lead	Pb	Tungsten	W
Magnesium	Mg	Uranium	U
Manganese	Mn	Zinc	Zn

Metal	Estimated life of known deposits (1972)
Aluminium	165 years
Iron	65 years
Copper	18 years
Zinc	17 years
Tin	16 years
Lead	10 years

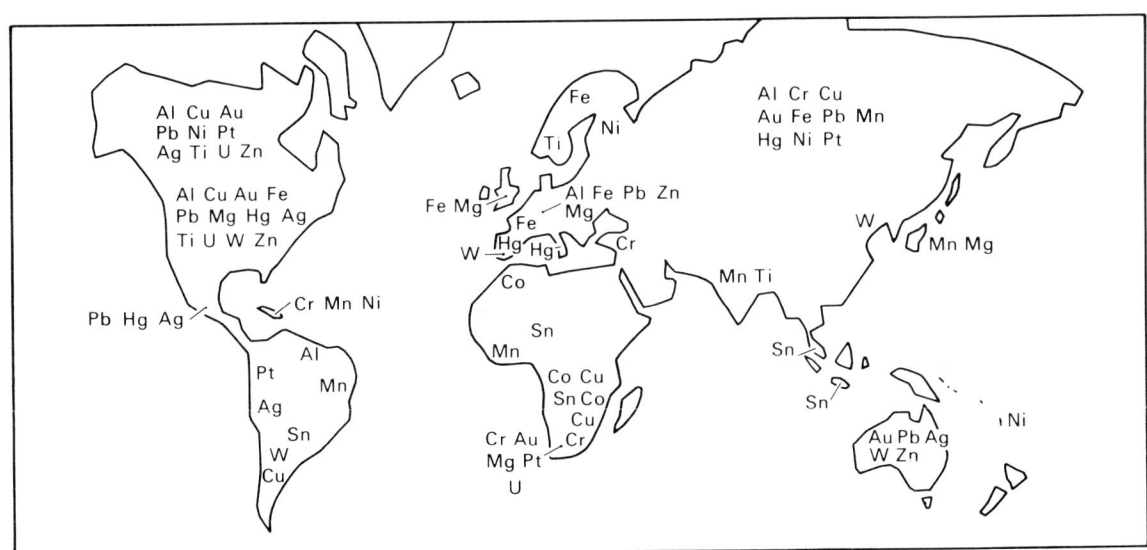

The table has great significance. It explains something about the high cost of tin, copper and lead, all of which can be extracted with comparative ease. As the cost of metal goes up, it becomes more and more worthwhile for mining companies to investigate poorer quality ores and extract the metal. This is what is happening with copper at the present time. The prices of metals in the world markets are changing all the time and are given in several daily papers. It is very interesting to look at the way prices change and, especially, to compare them with what they were five or ten years ago. In order to get an idea of this, look at the price lists and see which metals have gone up in price and which have stayed the same. Have any gone down in price over the years?

It is very important that we should find ways of reclaiming metals after they have finished the job for which they were intended. Do you think it makes sense for us simply to leave scrapped cars to rust away? Is it right for us to throw away tins? After all, when we do this the iron contained in the tins has gone forever. And the same is true of lead. Do we need to use so much

lead in petrol, when it simply goes out through the exhaust and pollutes the air we breathe? In this way we are wasting our natural resources. It is possible to use synthetic substitutes for metals, but these have to be manufactured in metal machinery. In any case, such substitutes are made from other natural resources, such as oil, and one day these too will be used up.

The figures in the table refer to known deposits. Geological and mineral surveys are being carried out all the time, looking for new deposits of ores that it might be worthwhile mining. The map (Figure 14) shows the distribution of major deposits of the common metal ores. You can see that a small number of areas are rich in a wide variety of metal ores. But other areas, such as Great Britain, are very badly off. But we must remember that certain areas have been much more deeply probed than others.

Certain under-developed areas of the world may well have rich reserves of scarce metal ores. This and the possibility—as yet remote—of mining from the sea bed represent glimmers of hope that we may be able to extend the years given in the table. But this hope must not

'As man's technological capacity has increased he has discovered how to extract and use more metals . . .'

Figure 15 A slimes dam at a South African gold mine

tempt us to ignore the unavoidable fact that eventually the resources will run out. Before this happens, the mounting cost of extracting poorer and poorer yields could cause us to forget about the environment. Gold mining in South Africa is an example of this and shows us what we shall have to avoid. Around cities like Johannesburg waste litters the mine areas in great mounds, which stand like monuments to man's greed and lack of thought. Figure 15 shows a typical scene.

In the years to come, as the fight for metals becomes more desperate, similar monuments might start to litter our own cities and country-side. To avoid this, we need to think about how we can conserve and use for the best the earth's rich resources that remain—before it is too late.

There are very real dangers for us in Britain. In past centuries metals such as tin, lead, zinc and copper have been mined in many areas. Old workings can be found in Cornwall, Derbyshire, Cumberland, Cheshire, Anglesey and Caernarvon for example. Perhaps you have seen some near your home or when you have been on holiday. These mines ceased production —and were left to rot and decay—because there was no metal left, or because the yield was so low that mining did not pay in competition with mines containing ores with a higher metal content or where mining was easier.

In a few years' time some of these sources may be used again, as metals from other areas become more and more scarce. And if they are, we must make sure that they are used sensibly and that the waste is not just dumped, but properly disposed of.

Aluminium: the New Metal

Aluminium is sometimes called the *new metal*. This is because only a hundred years ago, aluminium was rare—and therefore expensive. It is said that Queen Victoria had a tea service made of aluminium. At that time it was more valuable than if it had been made of silver.

But times have changed. Now only iron is used more than aluminium. A great number of everyday articles are made of aluminium now —frying pans, saucepans, cooking foil, milk bottle tops, toothpaste tubes. The fuselage of Concorde is made of an aluminium alloy called thiduminium. Can you think of any other products made of aluminium, or any other uses to which this metal is put?

Aluminium is now relatively cheap and this is one of the reasons why it is so popular. The great change in its fortunes has been brought about by two major factors. First, the discovery of a method of extracting it from the ore, and secondly the development of cheap sources of electrical energy needed for this extraction.

It was the British scientist, Sir Humphry Davy, who, in 1807, first suggested the existence of the metal 'aluminium' in the substance known as alumina. Davy was not able to extract it by removing the oxygen from the alumina (that is, reducing it), or by electrolysis, because of the primitive sources of electricity available. In 1825 the Danish chemist, Oersted, succeeded in obtaining a minute quantity but only by means of a very complicated process.

It was not until 1866 that Charles Hall in the U.S.A. and Paul Héroult in France discovered a way of extracting large quantities of aluminium. The process used today is basically the same. It involves using cryolite and large quantities of electrical energy.

The kind of industrial complex involved in the manufacture is shown in Figure 16. This factory of British Aluminium at Invergordon, in Ross and Cromarty, was opened in 1971.

It cost £37 million, and produces 100,000 tonnes of aluminium a year. It is situated near hydro-electric power sources in the Scottish highlands, and has brought much-needed jobs to an industrially deprived area. 18,000 kilowatt hours of electrical power are needed for every tonne of metal produced.

The occurrence and mining of aluminium ore

The basic ore: Aluminium is extracted from alumina, which occurs in crude form as the mineral ore bauxite. This name comes from the place, Les Baux, in France, where one of the first mines was developed.

Most bauxite mines nowadays are to be found near the Equator, in areas where hot sun and heavy rain have helped to remove many of the impurities, such as silica. This enables open-cast methods to be used. Figure 17 shows a typical open-cast bauxite mine. First the vegetation is removed, then the top-soil and finally any sand or clay over-lying the deposit. The mineral is then extracted by large excavators, loaded onto railway wagons, and sent by ship to alumina production plants in different parts of the world.

The colour of alumina varies from creamy-white to dark brown. The different colouring is influenced by the amount of iron (III) oxide present. The general purity of the ore varies from mine to mine. The amount of alumina in some ores is as high as 70% whilst in others it is only 50%.

The extraction of aluminium: The production of aluminium from bauxite is a two-stage process.

Stage 1 Alumina which is aluminium oxide (Al_2O_3), is extracted by chemical means from the bauxite.

Stage 2 Aluminium is obtained by the electrolytic reduction of alumina—that is, the removal of the oxygen.

Figure 16 British Aluminium's smelter at Invergordon

Figure 17 Bauxite mining in Ghana

Figure 18 A hydrofoil ship. Its hull and superstructure are largely made of an aluminium-magnesium alloy.

The process used today is called the Hall-Héroult process, after the two scientists who discovered it. Hall and Héroult discovered that alumina melts at about 2000°C, which is a difficult temperature to reach and maintain, but that it dissolves in molten cryolite, which melts at 1000°C.

The process of extraction is carried out in an electrolytic cell called a pot which consists of a shallow steel container with a lining of carbon. Above this lining is suspended more carbon.

Between the two layers of carbon is the cryolite, containing the alumina, and this is kept molten by the use of large amounts of electrical power.

The carbon lining acts as a cathode and the suspended carbon acts as the anode.

The reactions that lead to the production of aluminium are complicated and what follows is a simplified account.

The alumina (Al_2O_3) dissolves in the molten cryolite and produces what are known as ions, or charged atoms (a charged atom is one which has gained or lost electrons), of Al^{3+} and oxygen O^{2-}. During the electrolysis the alumina ions migrate to the cathode where they lose their positive charges to become atoms of aluminium metal.

Because of the high temperature, the aluminium produced in this way is molten and collects at the bottom of the cell. The aluminium is syphoned off, and can be cast into ingots. The whole process consumes a large amount of power, fuel and other materials.

Properties and uses of aluminium

Pure aluminium is soft and ductile, and has low strength. Cold rolling alters the crystal structure sufficiently to give it some strength. Research has led to the formulation of alloys that are very much stronger than aluminium, yet retain the other favourable characteristics of the pure metal. The most important characteristics of aluminium are:

a **Lightness**: Its density is 2.7 g/cm^3, which is approximately one third of that of iron and

Figure 19 Aluminium roof over Kidderpore reservoir at Hampstead

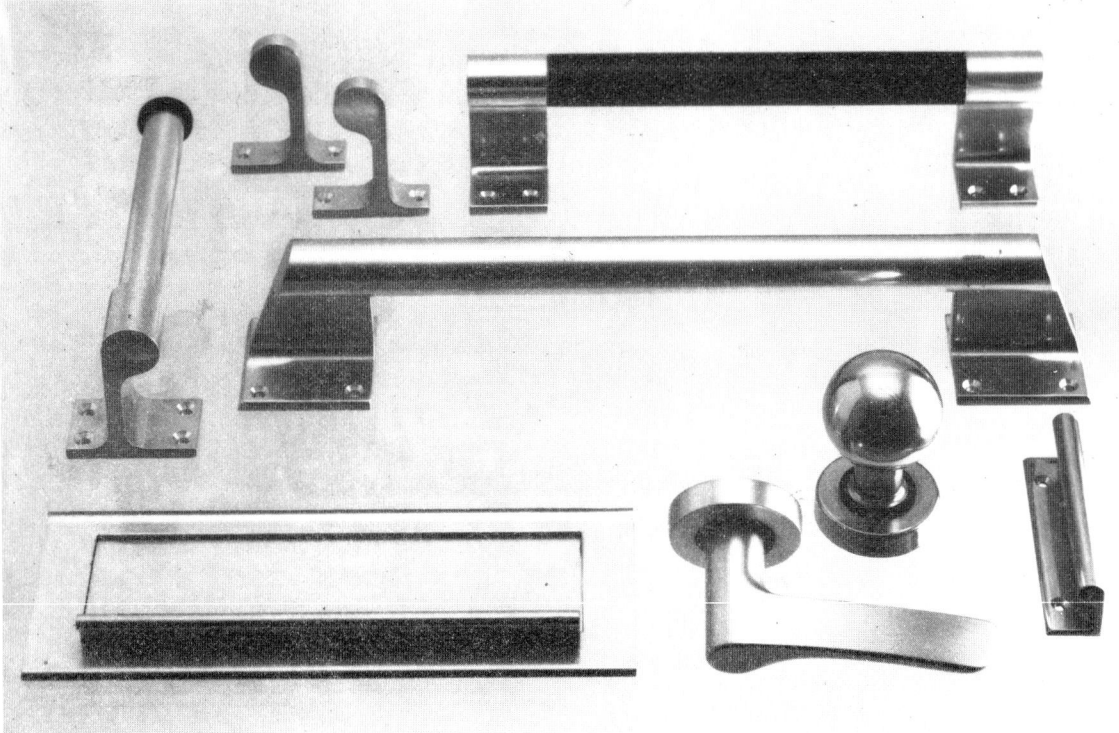

Figure 20 Made of aluminium

Figure 21 Casting aluminium

steel. Figure 18 shows a use of aluminium where this lightness is absolutely vital. Look also at the various other photographs showing aluminium in use and think about its lightness. In each of the various cases, do you think this lightness is useful, vital, or just another advantage?

b **Electrical conductivity**: Aluminium is not as good an electrical conductor as copper. In fact it is only 60% as good. But because it is so much lighter than copper, an aluminium conductor can carry as much electricity as a copper one twice as heavy.

c **Good thermal conductivity**: It is very commonly used to make food pans. This is because aluminium heats up quickly and evenly.

d **Durability**: As we have seen, aluminium is very reactive, but in use it does not easily corrode. This is because it quickly forms a thin coating of aluminium oxide, which itself protects it from further reactions and corrosion. This enables it to be put to the type of use shown in Figure 19.

e **Appearance**: Apart from the pleasant look of polished aluminium that leads to the kind of uses shown in Figure 20 it can be given attractive finishes, including anodising. In this process, the natural oxide film that forms on aluminium is thickened by an electrolytic process. The freshly formed film can be dyed in various colours.

The alloys of aluminium

As has been mentioned, the mechanical properties of aluminium can be improved by mixing it with small quantities of other metals to make alloys.

There are over fifty aluminium alloys, but the common ones are made by the addition of manganese and magnesium. If strength and corrosion resistance are required, then aluminium is alloyed with magnesium and silicon. For foundry work, silicon and copper are the alloying elements.

Figure 22 The train of the future—with a body made of aluminium

The working and forms of aluminium

Aluminium is shaped by the usual metal working processes. These include:

a **Rolling**: Cast slabs of aluminium are heated to soften them, and then passed to and fro between heavy steel rollers. Plate formed in this way is used for the superstructures of ships, sheet for aircraft, pans, and the well-known aluminium foil.

b **Extrusion**: Heated, round blocks of aluminium called billets are forced through a hole in a shaped die. The sections extruded then have the shape of the die. Many products such as curtain rails are produced in this way.

c **Drawing**: Wires and tubes are made by pulling lengths of rod through smaller and smaller dies.

d **Casting**: Molten aluminium is poured or forced into moulds, as shown in Figure 21, to make products for the car industry, or typewriter bodies, for example.

e **Forging**: The strongest and most complex shapes are made by hammering and squeezing the metal between dies on a forging press. Aircraft undercarriages and turbine blades are made in this way.

Aluminium is the 'new' metal—the metal of today, and probably tomorrow as well. The photograph in Figure 22 shows a use for tomorrow. Here the body of the experimental 248 km per hour (155 m.p.h.) train, APT-E, takes shape—in aluminium.

Copper: the Red Metal

As we referred to aluminium as the 'new' metal, then perhaps we should term copper as the 'old' metal. Man has used and worked copper (and gold, of course) since the dawn of history.

Copper was probably discovered and used so early in man's development because of the fact that many of the ores containing it are brightly coloured and therefore distinctive. It is also comparatively easy to smelt and work.

Man first used the red metal to make weapons and tools. You may be able to see examples at your local museum. Ask the Curator for dates, and see how the usage and ornamentation became more complex as the

Figure 23 Bronze ornaments from the Mesopotamian civilisation c. 3500 BC

centuries passed.

As the Greek and Roman civilisations developed, the use of copper became more widespread. If we follow the course of copper through the centuries before the birth of Christ, we can see that the present 'age of technology' is not so new as we sometimes think.

3500 B.C.: In Egypt and the old Mesopotamian civilisation, copper was used in burials— to hold the dead person's belongings and in the form of ornaments. This shows that even then it was realised that copper was long-lasting and corrosion-resistant, and that it could be cast and fashioned into all sorts of shapes. Figure 23 shows examples of these.

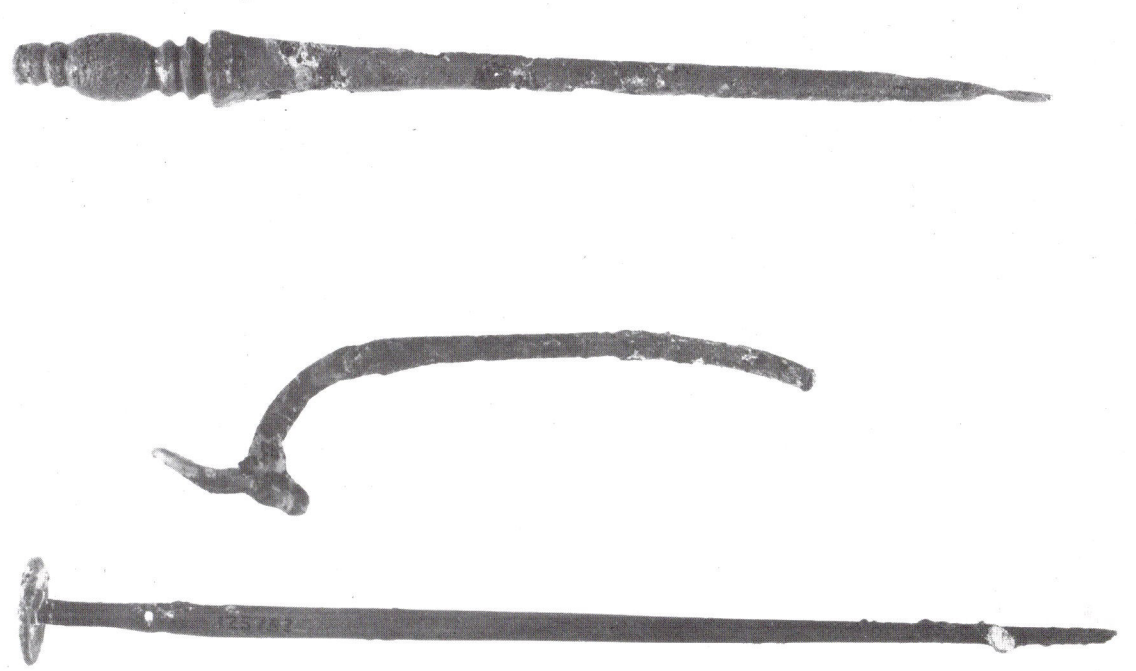

Figure 24 The copper roof of the London Planetarium

3,000 B.C.: The people of Ur in Chaldea (who are mentioned in the Bible) also buried bowls, pans and trays with their dead, and these are well-preserved today. The working people of that time had fully mastered the ornamental beating of copper, and had realised that it could be strengthened by alloying it with tin to form bronze.

2,750 B.C.: At Absir, in the Nile Delta, copper was used to make water pipes. When you looked round your twentieth-century home, as suggested in the first chapter, this was probably the most common use of copper that you found?

2,000 B.C.: The Middle Dynasties of Egypt, a most complex and wonderful civilisation, developed many uses of copper and bronze that we continue to follow today. Their obelisks had copper caps; bronze lamps stood on altars and in halls; copper pigments gave rich colours to their glass, and particularly to the blue-glazed pottery for which that civilisation is famous.

600 B.C. to 400 B.C.: The great Greek civilisation used copper and bronze widely, wherever permanence or beauty was required. They used pieces of polished copper as mirrors. The mighty Parthenon was roofed in copper tiles (compare with Figure 24 of the twentieth century). The red metal was also used to make coins and razors, as well as to make water pipes needed for their many baths.

Roman Empire: It was probably in early Roman times that copper was first alloyed with zinc to form brass, which is sometimes called the yellow metal. The uses of brass are discussed later in this chapter.

The occurrence and types of copper ores

Copper is relatively low in the reactivity list, and is found in small quantities as native metal in a number of mines. Except in the Lake Superior copper mining region and parts of the Andes, native copper is not in large supply. Copper is generally derived from ores which rarely contain much more than 4% metal and often less than 2%. The rest of the ore is

Figure 25 Open-cast copper ore mining

waste rock. At present it is not economically worthwhile to extract ore where the percentage of copper falls much below 1%. This situation could change in the future, as demand for the metal increases and the earth's store of copper ore is used up. The United Kingdom alone uses about five hundred thousand tonnes of new copper every year, and the United States uses about four times as much. This represents about 25 kg of copper per person per year in the United States.

There are many kinds of mineral ores containing copper. They are usually, but not always, found in mountainous regions where there is igneous or volcanic rock. The ores have a distinctive colour and are often very beautiful. Examples are:

a **Chalcopyrite**: This is the most common useful copper ore. It is sometimes called yellow ore, and consists of copper and iron sulphide. The purified ore contains 34% copper. About half the world's copper resources exist in this form.

b **Bornite**: This is commonly called peacock ore, because of its iridescent colours. This is also a sulphide and contains 54% copper when separated from the useless rock in which it is found.

c **Chalcocite**: This is copper I sulphide, and contains 80% copper. It is sometimes called copper glance.

d **Malachite**: This contains 57% copper and is a beautiful green colour. It is a form of copper carbonate.

e **Azurite**: This is another form of copper carbonate. It is a blue mineral containing 55% copper.

It was malachite and azurite, together with native copper, which provided most of the metal used in ancient times. In Britain, copper was mined in Cornwall, Anglesey, Cheshire, and other parts of England and Ireland for hundreds of years. Between 1854 and 1860 Britain was the world's largest copper producer. It is no longer mined here, but you might still find and collect

27

Figure 26 The working face of an underground copper
ore mine

pieces of copper ore in Cornwall, Cheshire and
Anglesey.

The mining of copper ores

If the ore is near the earth's surface, it is often
easiest to strip off the waste cover (called the
over-burden) and quarry in an open-cast
manner, using explosives and giant excavators.
Figure 25 shows this type of mine in operation
at Chambishi, in Rhodesia. You can see the
huge scale of the operation. It took one year to
remove 5 million tonnes of soil before mining
began. You can also see that this method of
mining makes a mess of the surrounding
countryside. This might not be acceptable in a
more densely populated country or, if it was, the
mining company might be forced by law to
restore the spoiled land to its original state when
mining had finished. Such restoration with
regard to iron mining is referred to in the next
chapter. Restoration is an expensive process, of
course.

The quarrying method of obtaining copper

ore is only practical at a few mines. The majority
of copper ore deposits are so deep that they can
only be reached by some form of mining.

The most common form of mining is to sink a
vertical shaft and cut passages from this
wherever veins of copper ore occur. These
underground passages are very large and have
railways to carry the ore from the excavation
face to the vertical shaft. In the Roan Antelope
Mine, in Zambia, the railway is twelve times as
large as the London underground. At one
Canadian mine there are 26 levels of workings.
The deepest is 1.6 km from the surface.

Figure 26 shows the working face in an
underground mine. The men drill holes into the
ore body and these are then charged with
explosive. After detonation the ore is loaded
onto railway trucks and taken away to be
crushed in ball mills similar to those shown in
Figure 47 on page 53.

The metal ore grains are extracted from the
useless rock in flotation cells which are shown in
Figure 27. There will be hundreds of these
cells in a large plant. The froth containing the
metal ore is called the concentrate and it
contains between 20% and 40% copper ore.

Figure 27 Flotation cells for separating metal ore grains from the waste

Figure 28 Electrolytic refining of copper—putting in the cathodes

Figure 29 A common use of copper

Smelting and converting

The concentrate is first mixed with limestone
and silica, and then heated in large smelting
furnaces, which are 40 metres long, 10 metres
wide and 4 metres high.

During smelting, the limestone and silica
combine with earthy impurities and float on top
of the mixture of copper and iron compounds
(usually sulphides), which are now called copper
matte. The molten slag and the matte are run
off separately.

This matte may contain between 40% and
70% copper metal. It is further purified in
converters where air is passed through the
molten metal for about three hours. Blister
copper is formed which is about 98% to 99%
pure. Blister copper is porous and brittle and
has to be refined before it can be used.

Refining

There are two refining processes: fire refining

and electrolytic refining. In fire refining the
molten metal is heated with more silica and air
is again blown through it.

Electrolytic refining is a more complex
process, giving a very pure product. The impure
blister copper is cast into sheets, which are used
as the anodes in an electrolytic cell. These are
lowered into a bath of copper sulphate acting as
an electrolyte. The cathode of this cell is a thin
sheet of pure copper. When electricity is passed,
the impure copper anodes dissolve and pure
copper metal is deposited on the cathode. The
whole process takes about two weeks. The solid
impurities collect as sludge at the bottom of the
cell. This sludge contains valuable impurities
such as silver. The preparation and scale of this
operation are shown in Figure 28.

Properties and uses of copper

Pure copper is a relatively soft metal with
excellent ductility. It can therefore be shaped by
the usual cold working processes. Its strength
is considerably improved by alloying it with
other metals.

The most important characteristics of copper
are:

a **Electrical conductivity**: Copper is second
only to silver as a conductor of electricity.
Michael Faraday's first electrical transformer,
which he made in 1831, was wound with copper
wire. Today, half the world production of
copper is used by the electrical industry. The
wires in your house are likely to be of copper,
as are the parts of the electric motors in any
model cars or railways you may have.

b **High thermal conductivity**: The 'best'
pans are made of copper or at least have
copper bottoms. They are much more
expensive than those made of aluminium,
Figure 29 shows a common use of copper in
cars, where the high thermal conductivity of
the metal is all-important.

c **Resistance to corrosion**: Copper has low
reactivity and is therefore resistant to
corrosion. Ever since its use in the eighteenth
century to protect the bottoms of ships (for

Figure 30 The copper alloy, bronze, is tough and corrosion-resistant

example, Nelson's *Victory*), its resistance to corrosion in sea water has been appreciated. The alloy bronze is also extensively used, as shown in Figure 30. Similarly, its resistance to corrosion has led to its widespread use in domestic water pipes and in industrial boilers, where it comes in contact with corrosive fumes. Its low reactivity means that it can be used for vats in jam making, whisky distilling and beer brewing.

The alloys of copper

As we have already seen, the mechanical and working properties of copper can be altered by alloying it with other metals. The most important alloys are:

a Brass: Brass has been used since Roman times. It is an alloy of copper and zinc. There are many different types of brass, with the percentage of zinc being as high as 40% in some cases. Brass is much more easily machined than pure copper.

Figure 31 Cast bronze bells

'Brass has been used since Roman times . . .'

b Bronze: This is an alloy of copper and about 10% tin. In this alloy the strength of the copper and its casting properties are improved. This means that it can be used as shown in Figure 30, where 20% tin is present. Phosphor bronze can be produced by the addition of small quantities of phosphorus.

c Cupro-nickels: These alloys form the base of much of our coinage. The so-called silver currency is 75% copper, the rest being nickel.

The working of copper

a Rolling and drawing: These processes are used in the manufacture of copper wires for electrical industry. This usage accounts for two-fifths of the world production of copper. Very thin copper sheet, produced by rolling, is used in printed circuits which may be found in T.V. sets and transistor radios.

b Pressing and stamping: Strips of copper and its alloys are widely used for pressing a large variety of shapes. Containers, tubes and coins are a few examples.

c Extrusion: Copper tubes used in domestic hot and cold water supplies are produced in extrusion presses. Curtain rails are often made from extruded brass.

d Casting: Copper and its alloys can be cast in various ways. The bells in Figure 31 were produced by casting, as are many of the copper objects you find in a museum.

Copper, the red metal, goes back almost as far as history itself, yet it remains as useful today as it ever was. Its great limitation is that it is expensive to mine and extract. Nevertheless, world resources of copper are dwindling as our demand for it increases.

Iron and Steel

Today and yesterday

Iron is the most common metal of all, and you can see it almost everywhere you look. But mostly you will see it in the form of steel, which is an alloy made from iron and very small amounts of other substances, such as carbon. In fact iron is rarely used as raw metal. It is usually alloyed to form steel. This is the great difference between iron and the other metals dealt with in this book.

The modern world is built from steel. Apart from being a material from which many things are made, steel plays an important part in the manufacture of other articles. For steel forms the basis of the machinery which makes nearly all our products. In this way, steel helps to shape wood, make glass, chisel stone and mix cement. The machinery needed to melt and form other metals and to make plastics is mostly made of steel. So just imagine how different our lives would be without steel.

Steel is the most important material in industry. This is why iron accounts for 90% by weight of all the metals used in the world today —because so much of it is used to make steel! As we need so much iron, it is fortunate that 5% of the earth's crust is made up of iron. Iron is not distributed equally throughout the world, but is found as oxide in large concentrated masses at, or near, the surface in many parts of the world, including Britain.

Much of the British ore is associated with geological deposits of the Jurassic era. These are found in beds extending southwards in a large crescent from the Tees to Weymouth on the south coast. The Northampton Ironstone Bed is one of the three main ones, and runs from central Lincolnshire across Leicestershire, Rutland and Northamptonshire.

There is evidence that ironstone was being mined in the Corby area of Northamptonshire in Roman times. The ore was obtained from outcrops or shallow workings, and was smelted with charcoal. This method continued for centuries, but the increasing demand in the Elizabethan era led to serious depletion of the forests. As a result, Parliament passed the Timber Laws, which restricted charcoal burning. Parliament was not only concerned about the depletion of the environment by the smelters, but also about the possible shortage of timber for boat-building, for a large naval force was very important for the defence of the country against Spanish invaders.

The occurrence and mining of iron ore

Iron occurs as either haematite (Fe_2O_3) or magnetite (Fe_3O_4). In Sweden, Russia and elsewhere there are mountains consisting almost entirely of these compounds. Such sources give an ore containing as much as 66% metal. In Britain the richest ores are those mined as haematite in Cumberland and Glamorgan, with a 49% metal content.

Our major deposits of ore are mainly of poorer quality, and contain only 20% to 30% metal. These sources provide less than half our home requirement. The rest is imported from all over the world, but mainly from Canada and Sweden. Though Britain's iron ore is of poorer quality and more costly to mine than foreign ores, we must remember that it is very expensive to ship ore to this country.

Most iron ore is quarried by open-cast methods, so we shall now look at the particular open-cast techniques applied in Britain. 83% of Britain's ore is obtained by this method.

The iron ore is found in layers of stratified ironstone running in horizontal lines between clays, limestone and sand, which are called the overburden. The ironstone occurs at varying depths up to 80 metres, but at present is only worked by open quarrying to a depth of 20

Figure 32 The boom of a huge walking dragline quarrying ironstone

metres. The actual thickness of the ironstone bed varies from 5 to 7 metres, but only the top 2 to 3 metres are of suitable quality for modern furnaces.

The overburden is removed by gigantic walking draglines. These scoop out about 25 cubic metres of earth at one time, swing it round, dump it and then return for the next scoop. This process takes less than a minute each time. The boom on the gigantic machines is 100 metres long, and Figure 32 will give you an idea of their size.

Both the government and the iron companies realised that ironstone mining would spoil the countryside, so in 1951 Parliament passed a bill requiring the iron companies to make sure that mined land was returned to its original state. This has led to the present situation where an open-cast quarry about 300 metres wide, for instance, can be worked so that the overburden is removed in the middle of the quarry and is then dumped at one edge. There it is levelled, topsoiled and returned to agricultural use— often within a year of being quarried. This procedure is continous as the quarry cut moves across the land.

Extracting iron from iron ore

Iron is obtained from ore in blast furnaces. These large structures are often 30 metres high and 10 metres in diameter at the base. The ore is fed into the top of the furnace with carefully specified proportions of coke and limestone. All this is then heated by great blasts of hot air. This heating, together with the air which is present, causes coke to oxidise to carbon monoxide and carbon dioxide.

Coke+Oxygen ⟶ Carbon monoxide

The limestone breaks down to liberate carbon dioxide and leave lime (calcium oxide).

Limestone ⟶ Carbon dioxide+Lime

The carbon dioxide produced by the limestone is reduced to carbon monoxide in the cooler parts of the furnace. The carbon monoxide removes the oxygen from the iron ore, that is, 'reduces' it. The amount of limestone used in this process can be gauged by the amount in the stockyard at Ravenscraig which is shown in Figure 33.

In the hot zones of the blast furnace the

Figure 33 Limestone stockyard at a steelworks

reduced ore melts and the lime combines with impurities in the ore to form slag. The slag is lighter than the molten iron and therefore floats on top of it.

The temperatures in the furnace vary between 1800°C at the bottom and 250°C at the top. The slag and molten iron are periodically tapped off. The process is continuous, and a furnace may be in operation for two years before its heat-resistant brick lining needs replacing.

After being tapped off, the molten iron is either charged directly into a steel-making furnace, or is first cast into ingots as shown in Figure 34. This iron is called pig-iron. It may be re-melted for castings. It contains about 4% carbon and smaller quantities of manganese, silicon, sulphur and phosphorus, all of which have to be removed in the steel-making process.

Making steel

The process of making steel is much more

Figure 34 Casting ingots

Figure 35 The open hearth shop at the Ravenscraig works

complicated and difficult to describe than the extraction of iron. Many kinds of steel are manufactured—often with a particular use in mind. These different steels are alloys of iron. They are made by the addition of carefully measured amounts of other metals or carbon to the iron during steel-making. It is not only iron from the blast furnaces that is charged to the steel furnaces, but scrap as well. To add to the complications, there are several kinds of steel-making processes involved. These have been developed over the past century, and are continuing to develop.

In order to be able to follow these processes, look at the photographs of the various stages in each one.

a Open hearth furnace: The open hearth process was developed in the 1870s and is used to convert both molten metal and scrap into steel. Figure 35 shows open hearth furnaces.

The furnace is horizontal. It has a roof of firebrick and a hearth at the bottom to hold the metal. The furnace is heated by oil or gas. Hot air is also blown in.

Limestone and ore are added to the hot metal and scrap. The ore liberates oxygen, which oxidises the impurities. These then form a slag and float on top of the molten steel. At regular intervals during the ten hours or so it takes for the charge of about 300 tonnes to be converted into steel, samples are taken to test and control the quality of the product. When most of the impurities have been removed, additions are made to give the alloy or quality of steel that is required.

Because the open hearth process is slow, its use is slowly declining in favour of the other two processes.

b Electric arc furnace: Unlike the open hearth and the basic oxygen processes, the electric arc furnace uses only scrap. Hot, molten metal plays no part in this process. Figure 36 shows an electric arc furnace.

The process was originally used for making

Figure 36 An electric arc furnace

steels of especially high quality, as it gave fairly precise control over the composition of the steel. Today it is more widely used. The furnace consists of a circular tub which can be tilted. It has a movable roof, through which three massive carbon electrodes can be raised or lowered.

At the start of the process the electrodes are withdrawn and the roof is swung clear. The steel scrap is then put into the furnace from a large steel basket. When this has been done, the roof is swung back into position and the electrodes are lowered.

A very powerful electric current is passed, causing an arc to be struck. The heat generated by this arc melts the scrap.

Additions of lime and iron ore serve the same purpose as in the open hearth furnace. Samples are taken regularly throughout the process, and these are analysed.

Once the correct composition has been achieved, the furnace is tilted backwards to remove the slag. It is then rotated forward, and

the steel is tapped into large ladles for casting. Figure 37 shows this being done.

The electric arc furnace can produce 150 tonnes of steel in four hours.

c **Basic oxygen furnace**: This is becoming the main method of making steel. Modern furnaces of this type can take 300 tonnes of charge at a time and convert it to steel in only 40 minutes.

Scrap and molten metal are put into the furnace, which is shown in Figure 38. Then a water-cooled oxygen lance is lowered into the furnace and high-purity oxygen is blown onto the metal. The oxygen combines with the unwanted elements from the molten charge and oxidises them. They then combine with the lime to form a floating layer of slag.

Samples are taken to test purity and the necessary additions are made. The furnace is then tilted and the steel is tapped and poured into ladles for moulding.

In order to get rid of the slag, the furnace is turned upside down.

The steel from the various furnaces is usually

Figure 37 Tapping an electric arc furnace

Figure 38 Charging hot metal into a basic oxygen furnace

Figure 39 Steel being rolled through a slabbing mill

cast into ingots. These can be worked into a variety of shapes and sections depending on what the steel will be used for.

Properties of iron

In its pure state, iron—as distinct from steel—is too soft to be of any great use. It is a reasonably good conductor of heat and electricity, but these properties have limited application, because of iron's relatively high reactivity. This means that it tends to corrode easily. It also has poor tensile strength.

Cast iron is not pure iron, as its name might suggest. It is an iron containing a lot of carbon, and is therefore a form of steel.

Wrought iron is the nearest form to pure iron. This has very limited uses—one example is the ornamental work seen in garden gates.

Iron alloys—the steels

Steel is an alloy of iron and carbon. The amount of carbon to be added to the iron is strictly

controlled, and it usually forms less than 1.4% of the total weight of the steel.

Other elements such as manganese, silicon, nickel, chromium, molybdenum and vanadium may be added to the steel. If these do not form more than 0.5% of the total mass, the finished product is called plain carbon steel. But if they do form more than 0.5% of the total mass of the steel, the finished products are known as alloy steels.

These elements may be added to the basic carbon steel to give steel with particular properties. For example, they may make the steel stronger, or more resistant to corrosion.

The properties of the steel are also affected by the size of the crystals forming the structure of the alloy. The size of the crystals is controlled by working the steel at high temperatures, and by controlling the processes of heating and cooling the ingots very carefully. The aim is to obtain small crystals, because slips or deformations can be more easily controlled.

The way in which steel ingots are worked is greatly bound up with the use to which the steel is going to be put.

Figure 40 Car body presses at Halewood

The working and uses of steel

To control the crystal structure, any ingot or slab length is treated hot. This may mean that the ingot has to be heated in a soaking pit for several hours, to ensure that it is evenly hot all the way through. This is particularly important if it has been allowed to cool after casting.

a Hot rolling: The rolls may be plain or profiled. The hot ingot or slab will pass forward or back through them until the required shape or thickness is obtained. The rolls can reduce the thickness of an ingot by up to 5 cm at each pass. Figure 39 shows steel being rolled.

Rolling produces steel plate for use in bridges or shipbuilding. Plate is also used for car bodies. Strip, rod or section products such as joists and beams for use in building are also produced by rolling.

b Cold rolling: This process is used to produce thinner sheet and strip for products such as cans. This has the drawback of hardening the product, but it can be overcome by cooling it slowly. This slow process is called 'annealing'.

c Extrusion: Extrusion processes are the most recently introduced methods in the steel industry for working and shaping steel, and they are still developing. Because of its great ductility, steel can only be extruded slowly.

d Drawing: Steel wire is drawn, either hot or cold, from rod rolled into section from billets or slabs. Cold drawing has the effect of increasing the strength and hardness of the wire it produces but it reduces the steel's ductility. The hardness can be reduced by heat treatment. The wire produced by drawing is used in cables for suspension bridges, and also to make cranes, fencing, concrete reinforcement mesh and nails.

e Casting: As we have already noted, casting is of limited use in the steel industry, because of changes in crystal structure that take place during cooling.

f Forging: There are two main forging techniques:

i *Press forging,* where the workpiece is slowly squeezed into shape.

ii *Drop forging* (a most spectacular sight), where the steel is squeezed into shape by a falling weight, which is raised and dropped until the finished product is obtained. Great skill is needed in turning and positioning the product between the hammer blows, so that the correct shape is obtained.

The methods of forging used today are really developments of the hand techniques used for centuries by blacksmiths and metalworkers. Parts of cars such as connecting rods, crankshafts and gear-boxes are made by drop forging. Figure 40 shows the press shop at Halewood where car bodies are stamped to shape.

A lot of research is going on to find ways of reducing steel's tendency to corrode. Every time you see a scrap car lying by a road-side, you must ask yourself, 'Have we the right to waste our resources in manufacturing products that corrode so easily, yet use up so much of the earth's resources?'. Also, 'Should we not get as much scrap as possible back to the furnaces, to save these resources, keep our environment pleasant, and reduce the necessity for disturbing pleasant areas by ironstone mining?'.

Lead: the Plumber's Metal

Lead is the softest of the common metals. Because of this it can easily be worked at normal temperatures without having to be softened by means of heat, and without having to be annealed afterwards. This fact will help you to see why lead is often used by plumbers. In fact the name 'plumber' has a lot to do with the metal itself. The chemical symbol for lead—Pb —shows that it is strongly connected with plumbing. Can you see the connection?

Man recognised centuries ago that lead is a very soft metal, and it was actually worked by the early Egyptians, who also realised that it is a

metal with a very long life. Lead pipes were installed by the Romans 2,000 years ago. They installed them at Bath, for example, and the pipes are still in working order.

For many centuries we in Britain obtained the lead we needed from within our own country. This is why many areas of Britain have historical associations with lead mining and smelting. But nowadays these sources are no longer yielding worthwhile ores, and so we obtain our lead from imported ores or from scrap metal. Many disused lead mines are found in Derbyshire. Figure 41 shows miners in 1945 at the mouth of a mine at Bakewell which they intended to re-open. The tunnel leading to the working was 2 km long.

Figure 41 Entrance to a lead mine in Derbyshire, 1945

'In modern mines the air is kept fresh and clear . . .'

The occurrence and types of lead ores

Lead ore is mined in many parts of the world, as the map on page 16 shows, but a few countries—Australia, U.S.A., U.S.S.R., Mexico, Peru and Canada—account for more than half of the total world output.

The most important lead ore is *galena*, which is lead sulphide, but lead is also found as cerrusite (lead carbonate) and anglesite (lead sulphate).

Lead makes up only about 0.002% of the earth's crust, but it is very concentrated in the deposits that are mined. Some ore sources contain a high degree of metal, but modern methods enable ores with a yield as low as 3% to be worked profitably. Lead is often found together with zinc, copper and other 'impurities', and it is obviously profitable to extract these at the same time. One of the most famous world sources is Broken Hill, in Australia, where this is done. For many years it was not possible to use the zinc found in this

way, but recent processes developed in Britain have enabled zinc and lead to be smelted at the same time. This process is dealt with in the chapter on zinc.

The mining of lead ores

We obtain some lead ore by open-cast methods, but most of it is extracted by mining techniques. Like that used for copper, the process for lead is highly mechanised.

In modern mines the air is kept fresh and clean by continuously changing it, and damping down dust when ore is moved. Mines are often cleaner and fresher than many factories at ground level.

Ore treatment

The ore is crushed in roll crushers and ball mills, and purified in processes similar to those described in the chapter on copper.

The process of froth flotation was specially developed to deal with lead ores, and has since been used successfully with other metal ores.

Roasting and smelting

The powder that arrives from the concentration is not suitable for direct smelting because it contains sulphur, and also because it would clog up the furnace. To overcome these problems the ore is first roasted. The roasting causes the sulphur present to be oxidised to sulphur dioxide (a by-product that is used to produce sulphuric acid), and the lead combines with the other material to form a lumpy sinter, with the lead present in the form of oxides.

This sinter is fed with coke into the blast furnace. This works on a similar principle to that used in the extraction of iron. Air is blown through and this oxidises the coke to produce

Figure 42 Lead bricks used as protection against radiation

carbon monoxide. The carbon monoxide reduces the metal oxides to metal bullion, which is tapped at regular intervals—a lead blast furnace may produce 300 tonnes a day.

The metal bullion tapped from the blast furnace is called base bullion, and it contains silver, gold, copper, zinc, antimony, arsenic and other impurities. These are removed in refining and are kept because they are valuable in themselves.

Refining

This is done in several stages.

a In the first, copper is removed. This is done by lowering the temperature of the molten bullion to around $400\,^{\circ}$C, at which point the copper no longer dissolves in the lead. It becomes insoluble, rises and floats on the molten lead. This process is called drossing.

b At a second purification stage, blasts of air are forced through the bullion to oxidise the antimony and arsenic.

c The gold and silver are removed by an ingenious process in which zinc is added to the lead, and the rare metals dissolve in the zinc rather than in the lead. The zinc floats on the lead and is raked off.

d Finally, the lead receives treatment with caustic soda to remove remaining impurities. This leaves a product 99.99% pure. The pure metal is cast into bars and slabs.

Properties and uses of lead

a Density: Lead is the most dense of the common metals and this, together with its high atomic number, means that it can be used as a shielding in atomic energy installations, as shown in Figure 42, and to make containers for radio-active materials. In hospitals, rooms used for radiography are lined with lead sheet. It cuts out dangerous gamma radiation and X-rays.

b Softness and malleability: As has been mentioned, lead is the most easily worked of the common metals. Whether in the form of sheet or pipe, it can be bent without heating.

Lead pipe is used widely in many homes, and lead sheet for flashings on roofs and gutter

Figure 43 Lead sheet on the lantern roof of Westminster Abbey

backs. This softness and low rigidity allows lead to be easily bonded to other materials, such as plywood, to form laminates, which are particularly good for sound insulation.

c **Resistance to corrosion:** Lead has low reactivity and is resistant to corrosion by many acids and chemicals. This is why it is often used in industrial chemical plants. Its use on roofs to give protection against the weather also depends on its resistance to corrosion. The bright metal darkens to form a thin coat of impervious oxide, which gives it a pleasant silver-grey appearance. If sulphur dioxide is present in the air, this will darken its surface without altering its protective properties. The lead roofs on St Paul's Cathedral and Westminster Abbey have lasted for centuries. Figure 43 shows lead sheet used in this way.

This resistance to corrosion and the fact that the metal itself is impervious to moisture make it ideal for use as sheath in cables. Cables across oceans or under streets are vital to our lives, and moisture must not get in—a lead sheath stops that possibility very effectively. Figure 44 shows cables sheathed in lead.

The alloys of lead—more uses

a **Antimonal lead:** The addition of small quantities of antimony—which is a silver-white metal—produces a harder lead that can be machined. Antimonal lead is used as the framework for the plates in car batteries. The spaces in the plates are filled with lead paste. This use in electric storage batteries accounts for about 30% of world lead consumption, and much of it is retrieved at the end of the battery's life.

b **Tellurium lead:** This alloy, unlike lead, becomes tougher and stronger when worked.

c **Solder:** When alloyed with tin, lead makes a wide range of soft solders. These have low melting points, and so do not affect the metals

Figure 44 Cable with lead sheathing

being joined. A solder of 70% lead and 30% tin is pasty over a wide range of temperatures and is suitable for use by plumbers, who have to wipe joints with it while it is still molten. On the other hand, a solder of 62% tin and 38% lead melts suddenly at 183°C to become a free-flowing liquid with no pasty stage. As such, it is widely used by tin-smiths working with accuracy and in small areas.

By varying the proportions of the lead and tin, and by the addition of other materials, a whole range of solders with a wide variety of properties can be obtained. Figure 45 shows a joint being soldered on a lead pipe.

Lead and bearings

Lead has been used for many years to reduce friction in bearings in machines and motor cars. It is used as lead metal, or as white metal alloy. In more recent times it has been used in association with plastic in the unlubricated bearings found in washing machines. In theory, these will provide a component which will operate for many years without attention or oiling.

The working of lead

a **Rolling**: Pegs of lead are melted down and cast into slabs about 12 cm thick. These slabs are rolled down to 2 cm and then passed through mills which make them even thinner. Lead sheet and lead alloy sheet are made in this way.

b **Extrusion**: Because of its softness, lead is easily extruded, and pipe up to about 400 cm in diameter can be made.

c **Casting**: A small quantity of lead is still cast for ornamental lead work, but because of its high shrinking factor, lead is not often used for this purpose.

Anti-knock

The second largest consumers of lead in the world are the petrol companies. They convert it

Figure 45 Soldering a joint on lead pipe

to tetra-ethyl lead, which is added to petrol. This additive reduces friction in motor car engines and allows them to work more efficiently. The waste passes into the air. In this way we are hardly using the earth's resources carefully and looking into the future, you might think. After all, our lead resources will not last for ever. Also this waste lead is obviously polluting the air we breathe, and so in this way we are gradually poisoning ourselves!

Gold: the Yellow Metal

Everybody knows that gold is a precious metal and therefore very expensive. This was why we did not suggest experiments for you to do using gold. But did you include gold in the list of metals around the home, and notice the kind of use it was put to? These uses have not changed for thousands of years, and are only partly concerned with its high cost. Figure 46 shows gold being put to its most common human use —the production of body ornaments.

Although it is found native—that is, as metal, not ore—gold is expensive. This is because it is very scarce on the earth's surface.

Many of its uses are connected with the fact that it has a beautiful, distinct colour and does not tarnish or corrode.

Ancient man very quickly recognised these properties. The great civilisations of Egypt, India and Peru adored gold, and gave it religious significance. The cult significance is illustrated, for instance, by Moses overthrowing the Golden Calf, Hercules gathering golden apples in the Garden of Hesperides, Jason capturing the Golden Fleece, Minerva and Baal being golden statues, and by a golden bough opening the door of Hell in Aenaes. In Wagner's opera, *Der Ring der Niebelungen,* the prestige of and greed for gold that have been perpetually associated with the yellow metal throughout myth and history are represented. Gold has often been condemned by moralists, philosophers, and statesmen, many of whom then set about hoarding it themselves. Hitler proclaimed that gold was decadent, but he robbed the gold stocks of the countries he invaded.

The earliest method of gold extraction was panning. Crushed material would be continuously swilled in water in a large, flat pan. The lighter waste material is washed away, leaving the heavier gold behind. This method, because of its dependence on easy access to gold seams, is very much a thing of the past. Such seams have been 'worked out' many years ago.

The mining of gold

The first problem is finding the gold. This is done by drilling holes in areas where geological surveys have indicated that gold might be found. If the geological survey is correct, and the borehole crosses a seam containing gold, mining goes ahead.

In the Orange Free State goldfield of South Africa, the vein containing the gold is found over a kilometre below ground. Even then, it is in a vein only 20 cm deep, containing pebbles and quartz, and sometimes at the bottom in a carbon layer only 0.3 cm thick. Considering these facts, we can begin to appreciate why gold is so expensive.

Shafts are sunk to the veins. This is often made difficult by the presence of sealed underground water at great pressure—and methane gas. Complex and costly processes of sealing the shafts as they are sunk have been developed to overcome this.

The underground systems involved in obtaining the gold-bearing rock are similar to those outlined in the chapter on copper. However, in some cases the height of the working face area is often little more than 1 metre.

Rock containing gold is brought to the surface for treatment.

Extracting gold from the ore

The gold occurs as tiny specks in the rock. It is separated by a series of processes which take place in massive housings, machinery and tanks which altogether cover several hectares of ground.

Figure 46 Burnished gold necklace set with precious
stones

1 Ore dressing

a Washing: The ore is taken from the ore dump
to the plant by conveyor belt. It is washed so
that waste rock can be sorted from the gold-
bearing part. This is often done by hand. The
waste rock is sent to a dump. Many massive
dumps can be seen near gold mines.

b Crushing and grinding: The remaining ore
rock is crushed to a size suitable for the grinding
mills which are shown in Figure 47.

c Classifiers: The ore is then passed to
classifiers, which separate sand from the finely
ground ore. These are now called 'slimes'.

2 Gold by amalgamation

The larger particles of gold are extracted by
rotating the sand in cylinders lined with rubber
corduroy. The gold particles are trapped in the
corduroy and are removed and taken to the
recovery house at regular intervals.

There the gold is milled with mercury to
form an amalgam. This is then heated in

retorts and the mercury is removed as vapour.
The gold bullion that remains is re-melted
and cast into ingots.

Although the amalgamation process is an
effective means of obtaining the gold, it is only
suitable for recovering the coarse particles.
The finer specks—accounting for 60% of the
total—have to be recovered by the cyanide
process.

3 Gold by cyaniding

a Cyaniding: Cyanide is added to the slimes in
large cylindrical tanks called 'pachucas' and the
gold dissolves in the cyanide.

b Filtering: This separates the cyanide
solution from the waste.

c Precipitation: Here the gold is recovered
from the cyanide. This is achieved by the
addition of zinc dust. Zinc is more soluble in
cyanide than gold and displaces it as a
precipitate.

d Roasting and smelting: The gold from the
filters is removed regularly and treated with
sulphuric acid to remove the zinc. The
remainder, still containing many impurities, is

Figure 47 Grinding mills as used in gold extraction

purified, smelted and cast into ingots, each weighing about 31 kg.

Gold ingots vary in purity, and a sample of each bar is analysed by the assay office. Their purity will vary between 90% and 94%. The bars are also weighed accurately. This ingot gold is further refined to 99.6% purity, melted and poured into bars having a mass of approximately 12.4 kg, and these are sold on the world gold markets. Figure 48 shows gold bars being weighed.

Properties and uses of gold

a Density: Gold is one of the densest of metals, 1 cubic centimetre having a mass of 19.3 gm. This is an important factor in the separation of the metal from ore.

b Electrical and heat conductivity: Gold conducts quite well, but its cost rules out any commercial usage of these properties.

c Resistance to corrosion: Gold has a very low reactivity and is therefore highly resistant to corrosion. It is not attacked by any of the common acids when used singly. This resistance to corrosion makes it very suitable for tooth fillings.

d Appearance: Because of its great beauty gold is commonly used as jewellery in its own right or as a mounting.

Alloys of gold

Pure gold is very soft and has to be strengthened by alloying. Pure gold is described as 24 carat, and the various alloys—usually gold and copper—are also described as carats. The number before the carat represents the parts out of 24 that are gold, the remainder being a common metal. The greater the parts of gold, the softer the alloy, and the more easily it will wear away.

Figure 48 Gold bars being weighed

The working of gold

a Beating: It is malleable and easily beaten into ornamental masks, a practice used in ancient civilisations.

b Rolling: Gold can be rolled very easily without any surface hardening. Gold leaf which is only hundredths of a centimetre thick can be made. This is sometimes used to impress titles on leather-bound books.

c Casting: Gold casts easily and accurately. Casting is carried out for jewellery and specific industrial purposes.

d Extrusion: Gold can be extruded into quite thin capillary tubes, which are used in ornamental jewellery.

Gold and the international monetary system

The international system of trading was, from 1816 until very recently, dependent on a system evolved in England, known as the gold standard. This system granted the right of payment for goods by gold. This meant that a country had to keep its issued paper or silver coin money in line with their gold reserves—that is, the amount of gold they had in their national banks.

Various pressures of inflation caused this system to be modified, but it still has commercial importance today.

Zinc: the Rediscovered Metal

Earlier we referred to aluminium as the 'new' metal, but we could just as well call zinc the 'new' metal. Unlike aluminium, though, zinc has been known and used for centuries. Nevertheless, it is only since the early part of this century that processes have been discovered enabling it to be extracted in great quantities. These discoveries have led to a widespread increase in the use of zinc and its alloys, for it is the ideal metal for a wide variety of uses. Using the modern technique of pressure die-casting, zinc can be used in the production of large numbers of complex, accurate parts. Such parts are to be found all over your house, and in your car. Items such as food mixers, door handles, carburettors and scale model cars are produced from die-cast zinc alloy. Zinc should really be called the 'rediscovered' metal.

One of the causes of this rediscovery was the question of expense. Zinc in the form of zinc sulphide is usually found together with lead sulphide in the ore sphalerite. Many mines, particularly in Australia (remember Broken Hill?), were finding that they had to separate the lead ores from the zinc ores and then dump the zinc ores in hillocks. This was not only unsightly—it was also a waste of money.

A great deal of research went into solving this problem, and the result was the discovery of the differential flotation process in 1912. This process revolutionised the extraction of base metals all over the world. The application of its principles enabled similar extraction methods to be developed for other metals, and thus has helped to bring about the world-wide industrial expansion of the last fifty years.

This new process meant that zinc concentrates could be obtained from waste dumps and used to obtain pure metallic zinc. The major process of extraction from 1914 till the early 1950s was electrolytic. This required vast quantities of cheap electrical power—usually hydro-electric.

With the increasing world demand for zinc, research led to the development at Avonmouth —near Bristol—of the Imperial Smelting Process for extracting zinc, which is becoming increasingly important.

We shall now look at this method in detail. In both cases, concentrates produced in a similar way to those outlined for copper are used, i.e. crushing, flotation separation and concentration.

1 Electrolytic production of zinc

There are four main steps in obtaining metallic zinc from the concentrate.

a Roasting: The concentrate—which is mainly zinc sulphide—is heated with air. The sulphur dioxide produced is used to make sulphuric acid, and the zinc is left as zinc oxide.

b Leaching: The zinc oxide from the roasters is thoroughly mixed with sulphuric acid to make zinc sulphate. This reaction is a typical acid base, giving a salt (zinc sulphate).

Zinc + Sulphuric $\longrightarrow$ Zinc + Water
Oxide   Acid   Sulphate

c Filtration: Here the zinc sulphate is clarified before being passed to the electrolytic plant.

d Electrolysis: The technique for the electrolytic extraction of zinc is different in several respects from that outlined for copper. Neither electrode is made of zinc, and the electrolyte flows in a cascade along a line of cells.

The electrolytic cells are lined with lead and the anodes are also made of lead. The lead is not affected by electrolysis and is not corroded by the electrolyte. The cathode onto which the zinc is deposited is made of aluminium. As the zinc sulphate passes from cell to cell, it becomes weaker, and the product—sulphuric acid—becomes more concentrated. By the end of the cascade half of the zinc has been deposited on the cathodes.

The cathodes are stripped every three days and provide zinc which is 99.99% pure. This zinc is then melted down and cast into slabs.

2 The Imperial Smelting Process

This process was originally developed as a cheaper process for the extraction of zinc than electrolytic extraction when hydro-electric power was not available. It was also more efficient than zinc smelters, which used sealed retorts to stop reduced zinc from re-oxidising. This process was developed at the Avonmouth plant of the Rio Tinto Zinc Company shown in Figure 49.

The process is still being developed, and is responsible for 20% of the world's zinc and 15% of the world's lead production.

'Items such as . . . scale model cars are produced from die-cast zinc alloy . . .'

Concentrate preparation: As with lead, the concentrate needs to be roasted to produce an oxide. This is then sintered to transform the grains into lumps suitable for the furnace. Lime is added to the sinter to help form slag in the furnace.

The furnace: The furnace is essentially a blast furnace, and is similar in design to a lead blast furnace. The lead metal that is formed collects in the hearth of the furnace. It is tapped periodically from the hearth, together with slag.

The zinc vaporises at $907°C$ and leaves the top of the furnace as a gas. This gas stream passes to the lead splash condensers.

The condenser: This consists of a pool of molten lead in which mechanical rotors are immersed. These create an intense rain of droplets. The zinc cools and condenses in these lead droplets, and dissolves in the lead. This mixture passes to the separators.

Separation: In the separators the temperature of the lead falls, and as it cools its saturation

level is reached. At this point zinc is precipitated out—just as sugar is from a hot water sugar solution when you cool it. The zinc, being lighter, floats on top of the lead. It is then decanted and cast into slabs.

Zinc obtained by this process is of Grade IV quality and contains 1.5% lead. This is suitable for a wide range of uses. It can be further refined and made purer by the vacuum dezincing process. This consists of passing the hot lead from the furnace, which contains dissolved zinc, through a vacuum vessel. Zinc is distilled from the lead and is collected in a water-cooled condenser. It is then 99.9% pure. This is shown in Figure 50.

Properties and uses of zinc

a **Density**: Zinc has a density of 7.1 gm per cubic centimetre, which is very similar to that of iron (7.9 gm per cubic centimetre).

Figure 49 The Avonmouth works of the Rio Tinto Zinc Company

b **Electrical and heat conductivity**: It conducts fairly well, but not sufficiently to compete with aluminium or copper. Its use is therefore not based on these properties.

c **Resistance to corrosion**: Zinc is more reactive than iron, but less reactive than aluminium. Despite this, it is widely used in the prevention of iron corrosion by means of the process called galvanising. This process is a very important one and accounts for more than half of the zinc produced in the world. It involves coating iron parts with zinc by dipping them in molten zinc.

Like the more reactive aluminium, zinc develops a thin, self-protecting coat of oxide and carbonate, thus protecting itself from further corrosion.

Electrical bonding forms the basis of an increasing use of zinc—cathodic protection for ships' hulls, referred to on page 13. Zinc slabs are connected to hulls and other pieces of iron-work which come in contact with the sea. The seawater acts as an electrolyte between the two metals. The zinc acts as an anode and

Figure 50 Pure zinc obtained by vacuum methods

Figure 51 Slabs of zinc fitted to the hull of a ship to stop corrosion

slowly corrodes away, but as long as some of the metal remains, the hull of the ship does not corrode. The slabs of zinc are referred to as 'C' Sentry anodes.

The relative cheapness of zinc and its reactivity factor—in comparison with carbon —account for another widespread use: the outer case and cathode of torch batteries. This is referred to on page 15.

Alloys of zinc

Brass is one of the commonest alloys, and is dealt with in the chapter on copper.

Alloys such as mazak and 'C' Sentry zinc alloy are produced by the addition of small quantities of other metals—such as aluminium, silicon and cadmium—to improve the properties relevant to their use.

Working of zinc, and more uses

a **Rolling**: Rolled zinc is used as a roofing material, and is capable of withstanding pollution.

b **Casting**: After galvanising, the casting of zinc and its alloys such as mazak accounts for its most widespread use. These alloys have been developed with the intention of permitting the rapid production of complex and dimensionally accurate parts by pressure die-casting. The toy in Figure 51 was produced in this way.

Pressure die-casting produces precisely dimensioned parts by forcing molten metal, under pressure, into metal dies. These dies are then opened to allow the solidified casting to be ejected. The properties of the zinc alloy allow good fluidity at low casting temperatures, and permit castability in the walls of intricate shapes. The die-castings can be put to use with little or no machining. The variety of the products of zinc alloy die-casts is great and

Figure 52 The body and fittings of this car are made
from zinc

ever-increasing. It ranges from typewriter
frames, food mixers, toys, portable radio fronts,
to uses in cars, such as seat belt fasteners, door
handles, radiators grilles and carburettors.
Figure 52 shows the car Zn 75 where body
and all fittings shown are made from zinc.

Surface finishes can be added during casting
—by coating the die—or can be added
afterwards.

Zinc is rapidly changing its image from that
of a dull grey metal of limited use—as it was
considered fifty years ago—to that of a metal
with many uses and a number of pleasing
finishes.

Conclusion

The Sunday Times of 9 December 1973 commented on the record prices paid for metals in London during that week. Zinc was costing £900 per tonne—an increase of 47% in one year. Copper at £1,112 per tonne was nearly 150% dearer. Lead was £328 per tonne, an increase of 140% since January. These prices reflect both the increasing demand of our technologically based society for metals, and their increasing scarcity. Even with these prices the report notes that it was hardly possible to buy zinc because there was none to be had. Yet it was not so long ago that man started to find extensive uses for zinc, much of which was lying in waste dumps at lead mines.

With prices such as these it becomes economical to extract ores with lower percentages of metal content (yields). This is being done. However, this does tend to mean bigger and uglier waste dumps for every tonne of metal obtained. Also important is the search for new sources of metal ores. Recent discoveries of copper ore deposits in Africa will certainly lead to an increase in the figures in the table on page 16—that is, presuming that our rate of use does not increase too fast.

In recent years man has tended not to worry about his ever-increasing use of the earth's resources. If copper was scarce or expensive for making pipes, for example, he would use plastic. Plastic was cheap and plentiful and much of it came from by-products of oil-refining. Oil is an earth resource, too. Like the metals, the reserves of oil in the earth's crust will not last for ever. Lately we have seen how oil has become both scarce and much more expensive. But before that, plastic and the materials from which it is made were also becoming hard to obtain.

Most of the metals which we use are capable of being re-cycled. That means being collected, re-melted and used again. It is surely better to do this than to keep using up all the metal ores we can find. Of course, re-cycling needs effort and organisation. That effort could come from *you*. Not only will such effort save metal, it will also reduce the environmental destruction that is associated with mining and extraction. That will make the world a more pleasant place to live in.

Doubtless man will continue in his search for ways to extract cheaply, and find uses for, some of the lesser known metals in the earth's crust—titanium, for example. Many properties of metals are not shared by any synthetic material. Thus, for the forseeable future, metals still have a vital part to play in determining how we live.

Glossary

Alloy Product of the physical mixing of metals.

Amalgamation The mixing of a metal with mercury.

Atom Smallest part of an element (all metals are elements).

Battery Source of electricity as found and used in a car or torch. Consists of two different materials, usually metals or compounds of metals, in an electrolyte.

Bonds Electrical links by which the atoms of a metal are linked to all their neighbours.

Cathodic protection Method of corrosion prevention by which pieces of a more reactive but cheap metal (such as zinc) are bonded to another (such as iron). The zinc corrodes more readily than the iron and the slabs are replaced periodically.

Corrosion Complex process by which metals react with substances in their surroundings. This reaction often produces rapid wear and weakness in the metal object.

Crystal Regular shape of the particles of a substance given by the arrangement of the atoms.

Density Word used to denote the 'heaviness' of a substance. It is usually given as the mass in kilogrammes of one cubic metre or the mass in grammes of one cubic centimetre of the substance.

Ductility Physical property of metals which allows them to be bent etc. without cracking. It is this property which gives metals their high tensile strength and permits them to be drawn out into thin wires without breaking.

Electrolysis Passage of electricity through a solution resulting in changes in the solution.

Electrolyte Substance which, when dissolved in water, helps electricity to pass by breaking up into ions.

Electro-plating Process of putting a thin layer of one metal onto another metal.

Extrusion The forcing of metal through holes (or dies) to shape it or make thin wires.

Froth flotation Process by which ground, powdered ore is separated into metal-bearing particles and waste.

Galvanising Process by which a metal is dipped into another hot, molten metal to coat it. An effective corrosion preventive.

Gamma radiation Short-wave radiation given out by some radio-active substances. Highly penetrating.

Ion Particle which has either a positive or a negative charge.

Malleability Physical property of metals which is shown by the fact that they squash rather than shatter when hit.

Open-cast mining Method of mining used when the ore-bearing rocks are near the surface. The covering over-burden is first moved away and then the metal ore can be taken out.

Ore Form in which metal is found in the earth's crust and from which the metal is extracted. Consists of a metal compound(s) and earthy (rocky) material.

Over-burden The 'earthy' material covering mineral ores. This term is normally used when referring to open-cast mining.

Precipitation Process by which a dissolved substance is made available as a solid by the addition of another substance to the solution.

Reactivity This is a chemical property of a substance. It is the tendency or capacity of a substance to form new compounds.

Reduction Usually refers to the removal of oxygen from a compound. It takes place in the high temperatures of the furnace with carbon (wood or coke) and carbon monoxide acting as the reducing agents. Important in extracting metals from ores.

Refining Later stages in the extraction of some metals from their ores, often involving the removal of particular impurities.

Sinter Lumpy material produced by heating coke with powdered ore. It is necessary to sinter fine powdered ores, otherwise they would clog the extracting furnaces.

Slag Formed in a furnace during the extraction of a metal from its ore. It forms after the ore has been mixed with a substance such as limestone and then heated. It consists of some impurities and waste earthy material and floats on the molten metal.

Smelting Process in the extraction of some metals from their ores. It involves the heating of the ore during which impurities are removed and chemical changes take place.

Index